My Journey

My Journey

A Life in Quest of the Purpose of Life

+ + +
+ + +
+ + +

ERVIN LASZLO

WITH CONTRIBUTIONS BY

Allan Leslie Combs	*Masami Saionji*
Jude Currivan	*Michael Sandler*
Amit Goswami	*Karan Singh*
Jean Houston	*Michael Charles Tobias*
Riccardo Illy	*Frederick Tsao*
Emanuel Kuntzelman	*Neale Donald Walsch*
David Lorimer	*Gary Zukav*

A LASZLO INSTITUTE/AITIA INSTITUTE NEW PARADIGM BOOK

SelectBooks, Inc.
New York

This edition published by SelectBooks, Inc.
For information address SelectBooks, Inc., New York, New York.

First Edition

ISBN 978-1-59079-518-7

Library of Congress Cataloging-in-Publication Data

Names: Laszlo, Ervin, 1932- author.
Title: My journey : a life in quest of the purpose of life / Ervin Laszlo ;
    introduction by Gregg Braden ; afterword by Stanislav Grof with
    contributions by Allan Leslie Combs, Jude Currivan, Amit Goswami, Jean
    Houston, Riccardo Illy, Emanuel Kuntzelman, David Lorimer, Masami Saionji,
    Michael Sandler, Karan Singh, Michael Charles Tobias, Frederick Tsao,
    Neale Donald Walsch, Gary Zukav.
Description: First edition. | New York : SelectBooks, [2021] | "A Laszlo
    Institute / AITIA Institute New Paradigm Book." | Includes bibliographical
    references and index.
Identifiers: LCCN 2021022018 | ISBN 9781590795187
Subjects: LCSH: Akashic records. | Laszlo, Ervin, 1932- | Life. |
    Consciousness.
Classification: LCC BF1045.A44 L38 2021 | DDC 133.8--dc23
LC record available at https://lccn.loc.gov/2021022018

Book design by Janice Benight

Manufactured in the United States of America
10 9 8 7 6 5 4 3 2 1

+++

*For Carita Marjorie, the historic-family Swedish-Finnish girl
who thought she had married a concert pianist—and has
accompanied me with love and care through all the post-musician
turns and transformations of my life.*

*And for Christopher and Alexander, our sons who
with their loving presence and intellectual
acumen made a unique contribution to the
unfolding of this eventful life story.*

+++

Contents

+ + +
+ + + +
+ + + +
+ + + +
+ + +

A Word to the Reader

THIS BOOK RECOUNTS THE PRINCIPAL STATIONS of a life that proved to be far from the ordinary. This, already, may be of interest to you, the reader. But this book is more than an entertaining read. It conveys a message that is important in itself and important for you. The gist of it is not, as you might expect, solely to impart the insights and conclusions the author has reached in his own life. The message is this, but not only this. It is also to highlight the importance of the quest to understand the purpose of life—of your life and all life on Earth.

The author of this book maintains that there is purpose underlying all the forms of life that appear on Earth and in the universe. The evolution of life is not a meaningless accident, something that just happened on this fortunately situated blue-green planet. There is purpose behind the evolution of life, and that purpose is not necessarily something decreed by a transcendental Mind or Spirit, although the existence of such a Mind or Spirit cannot be dismissed. Life's purpose, I believe, is immanent in the universe. It is encoded in you and me and in every cell of every living being.

This claim has a scientific basis. It follows from the realization that our remarkably complex and coherent universe cannot be the product of mere chance. More than serendipity is required to account for a process in which particles form atoms that form molecules that form cells that form living organisms. That random processes would have created the universe we observe and inhabit is astronomically improbable. In the time that was available for our universe to evolve from a condition of chaos to its current condition—13.8 billion years since the big bang—not even the genome of a fruit-fly is likely to have come about through random processes. Something other than blind chance must have been at work in the universe—something like a purpose revealed by the selection of preferred outcomes among multiple alternatives.

The idea of purpose evokes a negative response from natural scientists: it suggests the existence of something nonmaterial acting on material things and influencing the way they behave. This, however, is not an exorbitant proposition. The totality the Greeks called "Kosmos" is the womb in which our universe was born, and this quantum-womb displays consistent even if nonlinear directionality in its long-term evolution. The observed facts suggest the presence of a form of intelligence governing the way things and events appear and develop in the universe.

The Kosmos appears to harbor—or perhaps to actually *be*—an all-encompassing intelligence. This intelligence endows the processes that unfold in space and time with the tendency to create complex and coherent wholes: dynamic natural systems. The systems that evolve range in size and complexity from groups of quanta in atoms to groups of solar systems in galaxies—and groups of galaxies in the metagalaxy.

An immanent purpose underlying the processes of evolution is a reasonable, indeed a highly plausible, proposition. Searching for it is not chasing phantasms but looking for something that is real and fundamental in the world. On the personal level it is a highly meaningful quest, perhaps the most meaningful we could pursue in our life. And it could bring practical benefits. It could help us to align with the rhythms and balances of evolution in the universe. Seeking this alignment is saner and healthier than pursuing arbitrary goals of questionable validity and short-term benefit.

Let me conclude this note to the reader with a practical suggestion. Read this book not just for the entertaining turns and transformations of the life of its author, but for understanding the quest that it seeks to communicate. Understanding and adopting this quest could help you to find the purpose of your own life. It could endow your existence with the certitude that you are not here by chance. You are here for a reason, and recognizing that reason is important for you, and important for the world in which you live.

Introduction

Gregg Braden

BY ANY MEASURE, ERVIN LASZLO HAS LIVED an extraordinary life that has unfolded within time as well as outside of time, and the world is a better place because he chose to do so.

Through his life "in time," Ervin excelled in the skills of the temporal world to master multiple and diverse paths as a renowned concert pianist, philosopher, systems theorist, and teacher as well as that of a devoted husband and father. But it's from within the structure of these earthly roles that he chose to unleash his intellect in a way that was anything but temporal.

In a way that came to him naturally, Ervin followed the impulse of his "soul compass" that directed him, perhaps even compelled him, to think beyond the conventional boundaries of everyday life. It's this extraordinary act of self-trust that allowed him to live "out of time" and embark upon his lifelong journey to ask, and then answer for himself, the timeless questions of our existence: Who are we? Why are we here? Why now?

The Courage to See Beyond the Obvious

During Ervin's life in the 20th century, in many ways the world seemed more ordered than it does today, and daily life seemed to move in a clearer and more certain direction. While it would have been easy for him to be distracted by the awe of humankind's exploration of space, the technological revolution of computers, the biological implications stemming from the discovery of DNA's double helix, and the tsunami of scientific discoveries that emerged following the Second World War, Ervin chose a radical path instead. It was a path of honest inquiry that led him out of common time to think *beyond* the allure of the everyday world.

Ervin Laszlo had the courage to look, and allow himself to see, the dark consequences of the world's current trajectory, as well as the hope that a shift in thinking could bring forth a beautiful new world and our role in it. The key is that Ervin did so through the discipline of a systems thinker, tempered with the intuition and curiosity of an accomplished musician. It's this rare marriage of characteristics that gave Ervin the courage and the tools to search for a deeper meaning to the cosmos and human life. In this book, and through his lifetime, Ervin Laszlo is sharing his insights into the deepest mysteries of existence.

Several Incarnations—A Single Lifetime

In his own words Ervin describes how his life unfolded in distinct stages, including three phases of what he calls the "reincarnations," that form the framework of this book. Rather than the typical reincarnations that provide a continuity of experience from one physical lifetime to the next, the reincarnations that Ervin describes all happened through the course of his present lifetime. And while I have no doubt that the experience of the phases of his life may have felt as though they were distinct lifetimes while he was living them, I also believe that they unfolded as the harmonious steps of a single, continuous, evolutionary process. It's this process that equipped him with the vocabulary and the thinking to navigate the landscape of time from the perspective of everyday life, and also from the view of a cosmic observer.

Music, Beauty, and the Human Heart

Quite possibly, and I believe very probably, it's the mysterious power of music and the beauty that results from our experience of music that nourished Ervin's impulse to embrace the sense of a greater possibility for himself and the world.

Recent discoveries in the fields of neuroscience and biology suggest that our experience of beauty is more than simply a pleasurable aesthetic. Beauty is now recognized as a transformative force that allows us to shift what we feel in our body and, in turn, the way neurons "wire and fire" in our heart, as well as in our brain, to influence not only our health but ultimately the way we perceive our relationship with the cosmos. With these discoveries in mind, it's probably no accident that the first reincarnation in Ervin's early life created the foundation for his lifelong relationship with music and the beauty he experienced through his expression of music.

Ervin demonstrated the transformative power of beauty in his life through his success as an acclaimed concert pianist. In doing so he showed us that we can transcend the commonly accepted limitations of our own lives by replacing them with the harmony of a higher order. The desire to find deeper meaning in his existence and to contribute to the world led Ervin to the next phases of his life in the pursuit of how he would share his discoveries in a meaningful way. The reincarnations that followed were Ervin's answer to this question.

Philosopher and Activist

There is a timeless adage suggesting that once a powerful experience catapults us into a new way of thinking, it's impossible for us to return to the thinking of the past. It's impossible because we have been changed in the presence of the experience. We are no longer the same person. With this adage in mind, when we think of Ervin's life trajectory, it may be that his experience of beauty through the love of his music opened the door for the possibilities that crossed his path in life. And in the presence of those possibilities and through the influence of the creative forces within him, he could move only in one direction in his life—forward.

His next reincarnations reflect this fact as he sought out and successfully implemented innovative ways to express his deepening sense of himself and our origin, destiny, and the ultimate purpose of existence. His path as a successful author and public speaker allowed him to find the words to share his insights. His social activism allowed him to translate his discoveries into the meaningful actions of new educational curricula and social policies that reflect his sense of what's possible. And through his insights Ervin has given us a vision and a strategy to achieve that vision for what's possible for the world—and how we can become the best version of ourselves within that world.

It is probably no accident that Ervin Laszlo's life has unfolded as it has at just the right time and in just the right way to give us the right understandings precisely at the time in history when we need them. If his work had been offered at another time in our past, without the urgency for change that we sense today, his books may have been savored by only a small and dedicated following of visionaries preparing for the day when the magnitude of Ervin's thinking would be needed in the world. But this is not the case.

And this poignant fact is precisely the point of Ervin's life.

Ervin Laszlo's work is available for us today because we need it today. We need it now at this turning point of history when the clear and present danger of unsustainable thinking and living have paved the way for the global acceptance of his vision. Through Ervin's lifetime of writing and public speaking we now have everything we need for the template for healthy, new, and sustainable thinking.

Ervin Laszlo's Ray of Hope

There is a direct link between the way we think of ourselves and our willingness to embrace new and innovative solutions in the face of life's extremes. The neutral language of science gives us a place to begin, and the reasons to acknowledge in our minds, what we intuitively sense in our hearts—that now is no ordinary time in human history.

The conclusion of a 2005 report published in the journal *Scientific American* titled "The Climax of Humanity" honestly describes what we are up against as individuals and as a civilization. It's as current today as the day it was published and offers a powerful *ray of hope*, suggesting that if we can get the framework right, the future of humanity will be secured by thousands of mundane decisions. It's in the details of everyday life, the report suggests, that the most profound advances are made.

It is within this ray of hope that we discover the power of Ervin Laszlo's life out of time and his perfectly timed message of good news and possibility. We have entered into a once-in-a-civilizational opportunity to rethink the direction of our past. Thanks to Ervin Laszlo's dedication to unlocking the mysteries of our existence, we now have everything we need to make the choices and live the lives that can lead to the promise of a clean, healthy, and sustainable future for ourselves and for generations to come. Ervin has pointed to the path. Now it is up to us to choose to take it.

THE JOURNEY

The journey of my life is the story of the pursuit of a quest that is simple to state but complex to realize. It is nothing less than the quest to find the purpose of my life. I can say "my life" without being egocentric and blind to other lives because I am convinced that the purpose that underlies my life is the one that underlies all life on our planet—and wherever life evolves in the universe.

The journey that unfolded in the pursuit of this quest comprises three distinct phases. These surfaced in different environments and—except for my immediate family—in the company of different people. They were more than successive phases of one life; they were distinct existences of their own, veritable reincarnations. I call them The Musician Incarnation, The Academic Reincarnation, and The

Activist Re-Reincarnation. The events that marked each of these phases are recounted in the first section of this book.

The common motif running through all these phases has been the search to understand the purpose of life—of my life, and all life. This is not just a personal project limited to one person and one life. It is a project to be carried forward by all people who have asked themselves Why am I here, and why are we all here? It is the intent of this book to shed some light on the answer we could reasonably give to this perennial query.

My Musician Incarnation

I Was Born a Concert Pianist

THE FIRST STAGE OF MY LIFE'S JOURNEY was that of a child music prodigy growing into a renowned concert pianist. I come from a middle or upper-middle class family in the middle of Budapest who, by interest and avocation was considered to be part of the local "intelligentsia." This was a well-recognized and highly esteemed layer in Central and Eastern European capitals. In this setting aspiring to be a professional musician was a commendable aspiration.

On my father's side of the family, my lineage has been traced to the fabled Rabbi Loeb, whose extended and widely dispersed descendants included sociologist Karl Mannheim and physicist Albert Einstein. My father was born in the Transylvanian city of Nagyszeben and moved to the city of Budapest to study law. There he married my mother, whose dominant interest in life was music and had once been an aspiring concert pianist. Her brother, who lived in the same house we did, was an avid violinist with a deep interest in philosophy.

3

My maternal grandfather, somewhat of an exception in our musical family, was a skilled shoemaker who came to Budapest as a young man and within a few years created a flowering ladies designer shoe factory called "Graziosa Shoes." The factory was in the same house as our living quarters, and as I awakened each morning I heard the reassuring clop-clop of the factory's machines starting up below.

Music was the focus of our family life. A dedicated amateur string quartet met regularly at our house, hosted by my uncle, its first violinist. The piano could be heard at all times as well; I practiced for several hours, and my mother was playing most of the day. Her ambition was to be a concert pianist, but she had begun her piano studies too late to be a professional concert artist. Her shoemaker father had not launched her on a musical career when she was a child, and by the time she could have insisted on pursuing this career, she was too old. Competitively formed concert artists start their training by the age of five or six. The same problem arose for my uncle and prevented him from becoming a concert violinist.

When my grandfather died of a sudden heart attack, my father took over the running of the shoe factory. This enabled the rest of our family members to pursue their musical interests, free of the chores of assuring their economic subsistence.

My talented uncle was an agnostic philosopher, and his thinking left its mark on my thinking. A reality beyond the perceived reality, he believed, was a socially convenient and even necessary fiction—a convenient superstition and nothing more.

A set of principles are needed so people would live together without killing one another and ruining each other's lives, and the doctrines of religion furnished the necessary codes of behavior. My father did not share my uncle's philosophical concerns, and my mother was too concentrated on music to enter into them. My uncle had me, a young teenager, as his avid listener. Our afternoon walks in the city park across from our house made a deep impression on me, although I did not realize it until much later. I have never been inclined to accept any idea without further scrutiny, and my uncle's ideas, rather than being taken over by me, led to the clarification of my own ideas. Even if they subsequently needed clarification, my ideas have always appeared to come to me on their own, seemingly out of the blue.

My parents were keen on assuring that I have a good education. But they considered schooling mainly a formality that I, as a young concert artist, did not really need. If my school education interfered with my preparation for a career in music, it had to be tailored to size. The middle school I attended after four years of grammar school was a classical *gymnasium* and attending it did not interfere with my daily practice on the piano. The time and energy spent on my formal education had been reduced right from the start.

From the age of twelve, I was enrolled as a "private student" and was not required to take exams during the school year and not even required to attend classes. Instead, I had to pass a comprehensive exam at the end of each school year. I could manage that by studying day and night for two weeks prior to the tests. I memorized the answers, and after passing the exam promptly forgot most of them.

The schools I attended had a religious affiliation; the grammar school was Calvinist and the middle school was Lutheran. However, they were not chosen because of their affiliation but because they had an excellent reputation. (I found out later that John von Neumann and Bela Bartok were among the many illustrious former students of my *gymnasium*.) The schools were also within easy walking distance from our house, allowing me to walk over whenever permitted by my work on the piano.

My mother had already tried teaching me the piano when I was four but, as she later told me, this did not succeed: I always knew everything better than she did and did not listen to advice.

At the age of five I started regular training for a career in music. I did not read scores, just listened to my mother play the pieces I was to learn. I then played them spontaneously without asking what they were and what the score said about them. I was not emulating what my mother played, but picked it up and continued the pieces on my own. They were not new and unfamiliar—they were "recognized" rather than learned.

I proved to have such talent that I was frequently invited to perform at "house concerts" organized by eminent Hungarian families. One of these concerts was offered by the Baroness Elisabeth Weiss of the Manfred Weiss family, owners of the largest industrial complex in the country. From that point on, she took over mentoring my musical education. With my mother's enthusiastic agreement, she took me to perform for leading musicians at the Franz Liszt Academy of Music in Budapest. Here the world-renowned pianist-conductor-composer Ernst von Dohnanyi heard me and promptly enrolled me in his master class, although it was normally reserved for pianists at a high graduate level.

I soon became known as a "piano prodigy." My formal debut was with the Budapest Philharmonic at the age of nine, when I performed the Mozart Piano Concerto in A Major. Other appearances followed, both in recitals and as soloist with symphony orchestras.

The closing years of the Second World War created a hiatus in my career, but when the war came to an end and our family had managed to reestablish some measure of normalcy in our life, my career continued. I was named to the team sent from Hungary to participate in the international competition in the Swiss city of Geneva ("Concours International d'Interpretation Musicale"). This was in 1947, shortly after my fifteenth birthday. I received the highest degree of the Franz Liszt Academy, the Artist Diploma, the youngest person ever to receive it. In Geneva I was awarded a grand prize and was then invited to perform first in Paris and then in New York.

In New York, my debut made a sensation—The *New York Times* said that I had few peers among pianists of any age. Interviews and entire feature stories appeared in leading magazines such as *LIFE*, *TIME*, and *Newsweek*. I started traveling the world, accompanied by my mother, my tutor, and now also my manager.

The seeds sown by my conversations with my philosopher uncle were dormant, but not lost. In my late teens and early twenties they returned to influence my thinking and my view of the world. My life took an unusual and unexpected turn: It began to transform into a different mold. The roots of this transformation were not the fruit of rational thinking and design on my part—I seemed impelled to question and rethink everything I encountered.

Playing great music gave me an experience of wholeness and beauty, of spontaneously created and recreated perfection. This experience came of its own; I did not seek it or provoke it consciously. It came first and foremost when playing the music of romantic composers, such as Chopin. Soon I discovered that it is still more intensely catalyzed by playful works of genius, by music of an unspeakable lightness and wholeness. This provided an experience of perfection—every note was exactly as it had to be, unalterable and irreplaceable. This was my experience of the music of Mozart and Schubert.

Playing in public heightened the experience, but playing for myself alone gave me more freedom. It was the freedom of not having to do anything "for" or "to" anybody—just playing for the sheer pleasure of it. When I did, my mind could wander and my imagination could soar. I did not need to think about performing the pieces in my repertory; my hands, indeed my entire body, seemed to touch the keys spontaneously and this allowed me to feel and to apprehend all that "fell in."

Unlike most concert artists, I was not content with just having my musical experience: I wanted to know what it is. What is its meaning, and what are its implications for me and my life? One day this question arose for me so insistently that it changed my life. This was on a New Year's Eve at the Bavarian winter sport resort Garmisch-Partenkirchen. My young wife Carita Marjorie and I had decided to take a weekend off from our family and household duties. We were fortunate to have a Finnish *au pair* girl staying with us who took care of Christopher, our nine-month-old son, so we decided to bring in the new year in the Alps.

After attending the traditional New Year's Eve ice hockey match, it was nearly midnight when we stood on the balcony of our room overlooking the alpine valley below and the snow-covered peaks towering above. A determination took form in my mind that turned out to be not just a new *year's* resolution but a new *life's* resolution. For years, I had a profound sense that my life has a purpose and that I should be living according to this. But what is the life purpose of a concert pianist? To be the best pianist he or she could possibly be? Or was it something else as well? I had a definite feeling that there was more to fulfilling the purpose of my life than achieving success on the concert stage. Was the purpose of my life to experience perfection—in music, yes, but not only in music?

I felt that I had to look into the question of the purpose of my life seriously. Practicing four hours a day on the piano still left half the day for reading, study, and reflection. It was time that I settled down and became more earnest. I should be serious above all about my dawning quest to investigate what the purpose of my life could be.

My Academic Reincarnation

How I Became a Systems Scientist

THE COMMONSENSE WAY TO FOLLOW UP my new year's (or new life's) resolution would have been to take science and philosophy courses at a university. The University of Munich, in the city where we lived at the time, offered all I would have needed. But I postponed enrolling until later. First I wanted to reach down and understand my experience on my own. I had an intuitive sense that the answer was in me, if only I could uncover it.

Thereafter I combined playing on the keyboard of the piano with "playing" on the keyboard of my typewriter. I had a Remington portable on a desk across from my piano, and when all went well and the ideas began to flow, I got up from the piano and moved to the desk and started typing.

I did not analyze what I was writing—I allowed it to tumble onto the page. After all, I did not have to be critical of what appeared; I was not writing for anything or anybody else. This was a kind of automatic writing—of course, not entirely automatic, but not under conscious direction. I simply allowed my fingers to move over the keyboard. Being the fingers of a pianist, they moved fast—almost as fast as the unfolding of the ideas that appeared in my mind. I filled page after page and seldom read back what I had written.

Then the realization dawned on me that there must be others who have had similar experiences, whether they were triggered by performing music or by something else. After all, there are entire libraries filled with research on the aesthetic experience. I would do well to consult this potential treasure house and see if it would illuminate my own experience of playing great music and offer an answer to my question of whether performing music was the purpose of my life.

There was also another motivation. I was reluctant to share what I wrote because it was usually taken as nothing more than the hobby of a musician to fill his spare time. And when someone took my ideas seriously—which happened from time to time—I could not explain how I came by them. Most people could not accept that I came up with them myself, and I was ashamed to admit that I did. Writing without doing research, I thought, was naive and amateurish. Serious work on philosophical topics was supported by mountains of citations and references.

This concern ceased when my notes caught the eye of a gentleman I met in The Hague in Holland. After a successful piano recital, I was in an expansive mood and sat down in the buffet of the hotel with a sympathetic listener to talk about my ideas. The gentleman asked if I wrote down any of what I was talking about. When I said yes, he wanted to see my writings. I always had my notebook with me and went up to my room to get it. He started to read it and asked if he could borrow it for the night and return it to me in the morning. I agreed. The next morning he showed up with my notebook under his arm and said that he would like to publish it. He told me it would take some work to get my writings in shape to be a publishable manuscript, but he would help me. He then introduced himself: His name was Priem, and he was the philosophy editor of the noted Dutch philosophy and theology publishing house Martinus Nijhoff.

A year later, in 1963, my first book was born. It was a comprehensive essay in what I would now regard as metaphysics, centered on the essential nature of the universe, of life, and of society. Because I was a young writer publishing his first book, it seemed more modest to focus it on society, rather than life and the universe. With the publisher's help, we decided to entitle it *Essential Society: An Ontological Reconstruction.*

Publishing my first book made me realize that my ideas could be of interest to others as well. I decided to document them to make them credible and searched for books to cite as references. I lived in Lausanne, Switzerland, at the time and had no difficulty finding bookstores with a variety of new and used books on science and philosophy. When I browsed the bookstore around the corner I came across a heavily marked and annotated volume by B. K. Mallik who appeared to be an Indian philosopher. His book titled *Related Multiplicity* was published in Oxford in 1952. I scanned the book and came across the argument that everything in the world is an intrinsically connected multiplicity. This was relevant to my own thinking. I purchased the book and started to read it. It was the first philosophical treatise I ever studied in depth.

I hoped Mallik's work would help me with my queries regarding the purpose of my life. While his book did not give hard-and-fast answers, it challenged my view of the world. This was fascinating, and I wanted to go deeper. I found references to the work of the famous philosopher Alfred North Whitehead and went back to the bookstore to order his major work, *Process and Reality*. It was not an easy book to absorb, but my resolve to look for the purpose of my life was firm. I read it from the first word to the last.

Whitehead's philosophy did not immediately tell me what is the purpose of my life, but it further changed how I looked at the world. The world around me shifted from an ensemble of lifeless physical objects and chance-produced biological organisms to an organic network of interconnected wholes: in Whitehead's terms, the "societies of actual entities." The universe is a complete and perfect interconnected and interacting (and indeed, inter-constituted) whole. Things in it are what they are because of their connection to each other. Relations, not substances, are of the essence. All things are nodal points in a cosmic network. The network has meaning as a whole; all other things derive their meaning from being a part of it.

I began to see the world in this new and strange light that was also strangely familiar. I realized that nothing in the world merely "is." Everything tends, grows, and develops. It develops into, and develops as, an interconnected whole. This is true evolution. It is not evolution in the classical sense where it refers to changes in the gene pool of living species; it is evolution in the cosmic, universal sense—in the sense in which it grasps the constant and consistent transformation of everything in the world with and by everything else.

* * *

One day I was traveling by train along the river Rhine. I was headed to Beethoven's native city, Bonn, where I was scheduled to give a concert of four of his major sonatas. This was a privilege, and I should have been fully taken up with preparing for it. But I was not: I was in a different world. I saw the Rhine and visualized it not as a river but a "flowing." I saw the trees along the shores, and they were not trees but "treeings." The clouds floating in the sky were "cloudings." I found myself in a living, dynamic reality—a shattering, life-transforming experience.

I nearly forgot to get off the train at the Bonn station, and when I did, I reached my hotel in a daze. At my concert the next day, I had a shock. When I came to my senses, I found myself on stage in front of a distinguished audience. I realized that I was playing the second movement of Beethoven's Sonata Opus 53, the "Waldstein Sonata," but I didn't know whether I was now playing the principal theme of that movement for the first time or for the second time (this theme recurs at the end of the movement and then leads over to the third movement). If I guessed wrong, I would either repeat the entire second movement or leave it out altogether. What a dilemma . . . a decision had to be made instantly. I chose to move to the third movement. It must have been the right choice, because nobody got up or started laughing or whistling.

Later that evening I said to myself, this is not good, and it cannot continue. I can't serve two masters at the same time; I must follow my quest. I decided to leave a flowering career in music to devote myself to reading, reflection, and writing.

The opportunity to pursue my quest in a fertile environment was soon given. As it happened, a few days before the incident in Bonn, I received an invitation from Professor John Schrader, the head of the philosophy department at Yale. He invited me to spend a semester at the university as a fellow. He knew that I had no formal qualifications for joining a department of philosophy—the sheepskin I had on the wall above the piano was the Artist Diploma of the Franz Liszt Academy of Music in Budapest, hardly a qualification for joining a renowned philosophy department). Schrader said this did not matter—he had read my recently published books (*Essential Society* and the book that followed it in 1966, *Beyond Skepticism and Realism*) and wanted to have me cross-fertilize with similarly minded philosophers at Yale.

I decided to accept his invitation and went to New Haven, leaving behind—if only for a semester—my wife and child in Europe. As it turned out I also, and permanently, left behind a career as a concert artist. The second stage of my journey began: my "academic reincarnation."

At Yale, the environment was extraordinarily propitious for pursuing the quest that was the substance of my new existence. I met such illustrious scientist-philosophers as Henry Margenau and F.S.C. Northrop. I had access to any course offered at Yale, could meet any resident scientist and philosopher, and could audit any lecture I wanted. I took full advantage of this opportunity. I met scientists from a wide variety of background and expertise and audited courses ranging from cosmology to psychology. I asked myself, "What could they tell me about the purpose of life?"

Countless ideas were buzzing in my head, waiting to be committed to paper. But I decided to proceed systematically, starting with cosmological physics and proceeding to the life sciences, then to the psychological sciences and on to metaphysics. I devoured the books that some of my newfound colleagues had given me, and the works they suggested I have borrowed from the Yale library.

Before long, I started drafting a treatise I called "Notes on the Philosophy of Systems" based on the groundbreaking work of Viennese biologist Ludwig von Bertalanffy and Belgian biophysicist Ilya Prigogine. These "notes" expanded and expanded and became the book I published in 1972 as *Introduction to Systems Philosophy*. I owed the concept of "system" to von Bertalanffy, the founder of General Systems Theory. He reasoned that the simplest common term for the complex and coherent entities that emerged in nature was "system," meaning an integral self-maintaining ensemble of diverse elements.

Von Bertalanffy did not teach at Yale; he lectured there on occasion. I met him on one of his visits and we formed a professional connection that soon matured into a close friendship. He read the draft of the book I later titled *Introduction to Systems Philosophy* and wrote a brilliant introduction to it.

My new books were well received, and I received invitations from various academic sources. After a stint at the University of Akron in Ohio, I ended up as an Associate Professor and then Full Professor of Philosophy at the State University of New York's College at Geneseo. While teaching at Geneseo, I had occasion to gain formal academic qualification for my position: In 1970, I was awarded the title *Docteur ès-Lettres et Sciences Humaines*, the highest recognition then offered by Sorbonne, the University of Paris. At Geneseo, I was given considerable freedom to pursue my ideas. I did so, benefiting from contact with the students of my seminars as much as with my fellow faculty members.

Shortly after the publication of *Introduction to Systems Philosophy*, the wife of a colleague remarked at a faculty party, "When are you going to write something that people can understand?" That struck a sensitive chord—can people really not understand the concept of the universal connection between evolving systems? I told myself I must write in a way that makes this basic idea comprehensible to everybody. I went home and sat down at my typewriter. (This was in 1972, before the era of home computers.) Here is what the world truly is, I wrote. It is a world of evolving systems at all scales of size and complexity, from single-celled organisms to galaxies. They interact and create more and more complex and coherent natural systems.

It was barely a week later that I sent a slim manuscript to my publisher, suggesting that he publish it right away. Titled *The Systems View of the World*, it appeared in 1972, the same year as *Introduction to Systems Philosophy*. The latter took five years of thinking, writing, and rewriting, and this book had taken five days. It reached a sizable readership and catalyzed much discussion. It proved to be the tail that wagged the dog.

By this time, I was well launched on my attempt to develop a systems concept based on the revolutionary findings that started to appear in science, especially in quantum physics and consciousness research. I developed close contact with a number of like-minded research institutes, including the Institute for Culture of the Hungarian Academy of Sciences. I was fascinated to discover that some of my former compatriots were inquiring in a direction similar to mine, despite being dominated by the ideology of Marxism-Leninism, the official philosophy of communist dominated Hungary. I contributed several research papers to the courageous periodical called *Valoság (Reality)*, and was invited to give a series of talks at the institute.

Ivan Vitányi, the director of the institute, and several philosophers and social scientists working there became my close friends. We were fascinated by evidence that "information" is a basic and effective factor in the living world, and not just words and ideas created and communicated by humans. Despite the materialism of the official philosophy, it became clear that living "material" systems "run" as much or more on information than they do on matter and energy—they are dynamic, whole systems where every part is in close and constant communication with every other part. This I had learned already from von Bertalanffy, and then from Ilya Prigogine.

From Prigogine, I also learned about the existence of self-organization in nature, a process that leads thermodynamically (physically and chemically) open systems at higher and higher levels of organization and coherence. Later Prigogine received the Nobel Prize for developing the formula he called "the Brusselator," showing how a set of molecules create other molecules and relations by which they "autopoetically" evolve increasingly complex forms and levels of organization.

Evolution in the world of the living, it appears, "drives" in a direction opposite to the trend toward increasing entropy—the dominant trend toward disorganization in the material world.

We came across first-hand evidence that information is indeed an effective factor in the living world when we witnessed the amazing healing work of Maria Sági, a young researcher at the Institute of Culture. At that time Maria had just met the Viennese engineer-turned healer Erich Körbler and became his collaborator. Körbler performed seemingly miraculous feats of diagnosis and therapy with the help of a one-arm dowsing rod. He created a sophisticated system for interpreting the rod's movements. Malfunctions in the organism, he found, induce one particular set of movements, and healthy conditions induce another. Ways to help patients move from sickness to health called for applying a set of geometrical symbols, codified by Körbler as a "vector system." Maria learned to master that system and then went on to develop it further.

The original Körbler therapy called for applying the appropriate symbols directly to the patient's body by drawing it on the affected part with a pencil. Healing would then be facilitated by the modification of the potentials of the electromagnetic field produced by the geometrical symbols.

Maria discovered that diagnosis and healing can be effected even when the patient is not physically present. He or she can be represented by a photo, a drop of blood, a strand of hair, or another biological "witness." Healing occurs as if the patient was physically present. It also occurs by going back in time. This is helpful in cases where going to an earlier period in the patient's life helps to uncover the roots of a health issue.

I had many occasions to experience the healing produced by the information conveyed through geometrical forms. Maria has been checking, diagnosing, and curing the (fortunately relatively minor) health problems I had encountered occasionally. The information proved its effectiveness time after time. Yet on most occasions we found ourselves in different countries and even on different continents—Maria in Hungary and I in New York, and later in Italy. There was no known energy involved in these treatments, nor any measurable connection between us, healer and patient.

Over the years I came to a basic insight. The flow of information within the body and between the body and its environment is the principal factor accounting for how living systems keep or reestablish their health, and maintain themselves in the living state.*

The reality of space- and time-transcending flow of information has been confirmed in experiments carried out in the laboratory. Particles that have ever been in an identical quantum state remain nonlocally connected across any measurable remove in space and, it appears, also in time. Complex systems of quanta are constantly connected by instantaneous information. The same holds true for more complex systems—systems of systems of quanta, such as biological organisms.

The complex and coherent systems that evolve in nature are instantly and multidimensionally interconnected. I could affirm without qualms or hesitation: *The universe is a multidimensionally interconnected super-quantum system, nonlocally linking the complex and coherent thermodynamically open systems that evolve in space and in time.*

---

* Years later I developed this thesis in collaboration with the Italian epigeneticist and cancer researcher Pier Mario Biava—see our book *Information Medicine* (Inner Traditions, Rochester, VT 2019).

My Activist Re-Reincarnation

How I Became an Ardent Promoter of Evolution in the Contemporary World

I WOULD HAVE BEEN HAPPY TO PURSUE MY QUEST for understanding the nature and purpose of life in the world through research, teaching, and writing at the State University of New York College at Geneseo, but an unexpected invitation impelled me further. The renown brought by my writing and lecturing on the science and philosophy of systems led to the third-stage reincarnation of my journey—a "re-reincarnation."

The event that marked the beginning of my activist re-reincarnation was a phone call from Richard Falk, Director of the Center of International Studies at Princeton. He invited me to give a series of lectures for his Center at the great lecture hall of the Woodrow Wilson School. The topic was to be the international system. I protested, telling him I knew very little about the international system and didn't see what I could contribute. He said "never mind." He and his colleagues would provide the interpretation—what they needed was exposure to my evolutionary systems theory. I accepted, and delivered a series of talks on a world system constituted by thermodynamically open systems on various levels of organization and complexity, including the international level.

While at Princeton, I met faculty member Thomas Kuhn, author of the famous philosophy of science book, *The Structure of Scientific Revolution*. At lunch in the Faculty Club, we discussed my evolutionary systems theory as a general theory of evolution in nature and society. I called my theory "GET" (General Evolution Theory), following the example of the GUTs (Grand Unified Theories) discussed by physicists. I suggested that Kuhn's concept of "paradigm" is likewise a general—or generalizable—concept: it applies to various systems in nature and society, not just to theories in science. He agreed, and encouraged by this I began to develop the concept of "paradigm" in a wider, more general sense. This concept caught on, and since then it has been an essential part of my thinking, lecturing, and writing, the same as in the work of a host of like-minded thinkers and scientists.

My talks at Princeton led to an invitation by the recently founded global think-tank known as The Club of Rome. And that in turn led to my work at the United Nations as director of a program at the UN's Institute of Training and Research (UNITAR).

My path to the U.N. was paved by the publication of a book that applies evolutionary systems theory to the contemporary world system. It was titled *A Strategy for the Future: The Systems Approach to World Order*. It caught the attention of the founder of the Club of Rome, the Italian businessman and thought leader Aurelio Peccei. He asked me to produce a report for the

Club on the goals and objectives to pursue in the world system, following up the widely read Report on *The Limits to Growth* in 1972. This was a major challenge, and I accepted, although I was concerned that I did not have access to the resources needed to carry it off.

Peccei said that my problem could be solved. He called Davidson Nicol, the Executive Director of UNITAR, the United Nations Institute for Training and Research. Nicol promptly offered me to come to the institute as a Special Fellow. I accepted and moved to New York. I had an office at the United Nations, a secretary and, above all, the means to communicate with well-nigh any researcher in this field. (In the era prior to the world-wide information-communication revolution, working for the U.N. opened precious channels of communication that were not generally available.)

I worked for the United Nations for seven years. I realized the enormous difficulties faced by that organization in fulfilling its mandate and suggested that the difficulty resided in having to bridge the gap between reality and aspiration. Today's political reality consists of nation-states that consider themselves sovereign and autonomous, cooperating only if they wish, and they wish to cooperate only if it serves their own interests. The leap from the nation-state to the global level is too big. The solution, I suggested, is to create an intermediate level of organization: the regional/interregional level.

With the support of then Secretary-General Kurt Waldheim, I created a program at UNITAR named the "Programme on Regional and Interregional Cooperation." It brought together several dozen social and political science institutes in various parts of the world, and was served by a small but dedicated group of mostly young collaborators in New York. Our findings have been published in the NIEO (New International Economic Order) Library, created on my prompting by Pergamon Press, a publishing house in Oxford headed by the controversial media magnate Robert Maxwell.

At the termination of the Programme on Regional and Interregional Cooperation I had in hand a Declaration signed by eminent personalities from many regions of the so-called Third World. It was ready to be communicated by the Secretary-General to the General Assembly. There was, however, a technical hitch: Such a proposal could only be "recognized" by the Secretary-General if it came from the head of research at the UN system, an Under-Secretary General. It so happened that the newly-appointed Under-Secretary did not want to promote a project that ran under the aegis of his predecessor. Javier Perez de Cuellar, the Secretary General who had taken office after Waldheim, expressed to me his regrets. He read the declaration and was ready to endorse it, but because of the failure of the new Under-Secretary to hand it to him, he could not "recognize" it. In consequence, the declaration has never been formally proclaimed. This was a disappointment but not a complete fiasco. Several influential ambassadors to the UN had a copy of the declaration and many heads of agencies did as well. In the following years the spirit of the declaration, and sometimes even its letter, found its way to inspire some effective developments. New treaties and even organizations have been created on the regional and interregional level, and existing programs have been revised and revitalized.

I left the UN and retired to our family retreat in the hills of Tuscany. This was to be a year of repose and renewal, taking a fresh breath and turning over a new leaf. But that "sabbatical year," starting in 1984, did not end after a year—and to this day, it has not ended.

My sabbatical proved to be an extended period of active and intense work. I became affiliated with the United Nations University (UNU) headquartered in Tokyo and was named science advisor to Federico Mayor, the Director-General of UNESCO. I was keen to set forth my work for the Club of Rome as well, but this ambition did not work out. I proposed to reform the direction taken by the Club of Rome, since its one hundred members, mainly business leaders and politicians, did not succeed in reaching the heart and the spirit of society at large. New members, closer to the people, were needed. The leaders of the Club did not accept my recommendations and kept steadfast to their established orientation.

I decided to create a new think tank that brings together not just political and business leaders, but also writers and artists and spiritually minded people in all walks of life. With the help of a friend from the Hungarian Academy of Science's Institute for Culture, we called together an international consultative meeting that gave birth to the organization we decided to call The Club of Budapest.

There was a major difference in vision and aspiration between the two clubs. The Club of Rome wished to influence the way the world works by calling to task its political leaders. The Club of Budapest proceeded on the assumption that progress toward a better world called for the active involvement of people not only in politics, but close to the heart of society. The requirement, I said, was to create a club of charismatic people who could touch the mind and the heart of people in societies developed and developing alike.

In a surprisingly short time, the Club of Budapest succeeded in bringing together the leaders whose thinking makes a difference in the contemporary world. They included the Dalai Lama, whom I had the privilege to have as a coauthor in the drafting the "Manifesto on the Spirit of Planetary Consciousness"; and the world-renowned violinist Yehudi Menuhin; the equally renowned Swedish actress Liv Ullman; and the illustrious playwright, actor and writer Peter Ustinov. Soon two visionary national presidents joined as members: Czech President Vaclav Havel and Hungarian President Arpad Göncz. The historic figure Mikhail Gorbachev (by then out of office and devoting himself to the reform of world politics) followed soon thereafter.

Today, The Club of Budapest and The Laszlo Institute of New Paradigm Research (the institute I founded to research the new paradigm in science and society) provide the practical basis of my evolutionary activism. With the ongoing leadership of Maria Sági and an eminent Board of Trustees, the club holds international meetings and offers outspoken Declarations. The Laszlo Institute, in turn, researches the scientific foundation of the paradigm emerging at the cutting edge of the sciences and applies it to the problems faced by the human community. Its small but dedicated staff is directed by Györgyi Szabo and Alexander Laszlo, working with Nora Csiszar, Kingsley L. Dennis, William Stranger, Gianni Lodi, and Giacomo Brucciani. They are advised by eminent personalities such as Emanuel Kuntzelman, Pier Mario Biava, and Riccardo Illy. My elder son Christopher Laszlo oversees the principal outlays and investments of the Institute, and visionary Chinese businessman Frederick Tsao co-hosts with me the institute's New Paradigm series of books published by SelectBooks of New York.

In all these activities and projects, I am guided by a set of principles that spell out my basic objectives. They constitute my Credo. I offer them here since they may be of value to other evolutionary activists intending to make a conscious and responsible impact on the developments that decide the future of our world.

My Nine-Point Credo

1. I am one of the highest, most evolved manifestations of the evolutionary impulse toward coherence and wholeness in the world. The cosmic impetus that creates complex and coherent systems in the world is the ground and the guide of my conscious activism.

2. I am conscious of being part of the human family, and that the human family is part of me. Together with my fellow humans, I am coherent and I am whole.

3. I recognize that there are no absolute separations between people, only gradients of difference that help

us distinguish one person from another. There are no "others" in this world: we are all part of the same human family. The separate identity we attach to people is merely a convenient convention to facilitate our interaction with them.

4. Attempting to gain my advantage through no-holds-barred win or lose competition is a grievous error. It could harm the integrity of the system of which both I and my competitors are a part. When I harm my competitors, I harm myself.

5. Collaboration is the royal road to the wholeness which is the precondition of health and well-being in the living world. Collaboration calls for empathy and solidarity, and ultimately for unconditional love among the collaborators.

6. Ensuring my and my country's security by arms and other violent means is a self-defeating enterprise. Patriotism, if it aims to eliminate adversaries by force, and heroism, if it involves violence, are flawed aspirations. Patriots and heroes who brandish a sword or rely on arms are not defenses against an enemy; they are themselves the enemy—a weapon intended to hurt or kill is a threat to all, including those who wield it. Comprehension, conciliation and forgiveness are sign of courage and not of weakness.

7. Only the persistence and evolution of the wholeness of the community of life on Earth has intrinsic value. Material objects and the energies and substances they harbor or generate only have instrumental value—value only insofar as they contribute to the good of the whole of which they are a part. As exclusively "mine," a material resource commandeers part of the resources all people in the human family need to live and thrive.

8. Sharing enhances the community of life, while the acts of possessing and accumulating create demarcation, invite competition, and fuel envy. The share-society is the norm for the communities of life on the planet; the have-society is typical only of modern-day humanity and is an aberration.

9. I have been part of a wide-ranging aberration in the conduct of life on this planet, and I must now join together with all conscious and responsible individuals to overcome this aberration. Dedicating my creativity, energies, and time to this task is my inexorable duty as a conscious member of the community of life on this planet.

REFLECTIONS

*M*y life's journey, according to the preceding account, has not been monotonous. It has been replete with surprises and disruptions—bifurcation points that lead beyond the established conditions. There have been surprising developments, veritable turning points where the old has ceded to the new, and the new has proved to be radically different from the old. I call these bifurcation point "reincarnations."

Now, before reflecting on the insights generated by my multiple incarnations, I propose to take a closer look at these turning points and ask what they were and how they have come about.

A Closer Look at
My Reincarnations

IN ITS USUAL MEANING, REINCARNATION TAKES PLACE when a person who is no longer alive enters into and inhabits a different living body. The subject does not know that he or she lives in a different body; he or she does not "remember" life in the previous body. This loss of memory is a classical feature of the doctrine of reincarnation. Plato called it *anamnesis*.

How can we know that we have already lived a previous life in a different body? Although with some exceptions, we do not remember having lived an earlier life, in cases suggestive of reincarnation, *anamnesis* is not complete: We recall objects, persons, and incidents from a previous life. These perceptions occur at times and in places that preclude the possibility we have encountered them in our current lifetime. The sensation of recognizing things, objects, or events we could not have encountered in our current life is known as the experience of *déjà vu*.

This anomalous recollection-experience is widespread; most people have it sometime in their life. In some remarkable instances the person—often a child—firmly believes himself or herself to be a different person. And in some cases, the existence of the recalled person and the recalled events can be verified. The recalled people really lived, and the recalled events really took place, although at a different time and place.*

In other cases, reincarnation does not await the physical demise of a person. In these less frequent, but likewise often documented cases, the previous personality enters the personality of the living person and may even take over his or her personality. In esoteric literature, these are said to be cases of possession. Because of the disturbance this creates for the experiencing person, often great effort is made to get rid of the unwelcome personality, perhaps by engaging a priest or other saintly person to help the person in distress, or a desperate attempt, calling in an "exorcist."

None of these situations have come about in my life. I had some *déjà vu* experiences, but not significantly more than most people. And I have never been "possessed" by an alien personality. Why do I say, then, that I've had various "reincarnations" during my life? The reason is the curious shift—in fact—two shifts, that took place in my self-identity.

Normally, a healthy person has a single identity throughout his or her life. Multiple identities signify a serious psychic disturbance and have a dramatic effect, as illustrated in Robert Louis Stevenson's famous story of Dr. Jekyll and Mr. Hyde. Yet multiple personalities, if they come about successively and do

---

* University of Virginia psychologist Ian Stevenson collected thousands of cases of reported reincarnation. His most famous work is the 2,268-page, two-volume *Reincarnation and Biology: A Contribution to the Etiology of Birthmarks and Birth Defects* (1997).

not produce disorientation, are not negative occurrences. They could indicate a potentially healthy transformation, a maturing of the personality. Such transformations may be continuous and consistent, and do not bother the psychic equilibrium of the person. His or her personality is enlarged, but not damaged or replaced. I believe that this is what took place in my case.

Even if healthy and constructive, within-lifetime transformations of personality are radical. A new identity is born, with the old identity replaced by another. This is what happened to me, not just once, but twice. First I had the typical identity of a concert artist with ambitions and aspirations focused on public piano performances. I could not imagine doing, or even wanting to do, anything else in my life—certainly not as a profession, a mission, or a way of gaining my livelihood.

Yet I have many vivid recollections of my earlier reincarnations. However, these recollections are not truly "memories" because the events I recalled did not happen to "me". They were things experienced by someone I saw in my dreams or in a film or were things I read about in a novel. They did not cancel or seriously bring into question my newly expanded identity.

My musician identity has vanished; it was first replaced by the identity of an academic. Writing was the principal objective of the new personality, producing books and papers to create credible theories of who we are, and what the world is around us.

Communicating my ideas was the corollary aspiration, but it was not the end, only the means to an end. Teaching, preferably in the form of free-flowing seminars where I had the opportunity to learn from exchanges with my students, was the means by which I could reach a better understanding of myself, of the world, and of my role and purpose in the world.

In this academic stage of my life, my concert pianist identity was not just absent; it was a puzzle. I could not understand why I would have it in the first place. I could not fathom why my basic objective in life would be to sit on a stage and play the piano for a group of listeners.

Of course, the experience of playing music for people brought its own rewards. It was an enhanced-intensity experience that was very meaningful and gratifying. It proved to be the source of the ideas I had elaborated in my writings. But playing the piano for myself in the privacy of my own home was an equally strong experience and certainly much simpler to achieve than giving concerts. All it called for was a good piano and the peace and quiet to play it to my heart's content.

The attraction of the applause and the accolades that come to a celebrated concert artist had lost their magic. When asked if I miss the profession of a musician, I can honestly reply that I do not—much to the astonishment of my music-lover interlocutors.

My third-stage of identity replaced also the academic identity of the second stage. The aspiration to communicate what I thought and put into words had a new motivation. It was to make a difference to the life and thinking of those with whom I communicated, and through them, to the world. I was, and still am, awed and all but overwhelmed by the enormity of the challenges that confront us. I have been, and remain to this day, "driven" by the urgency to find effective solutions—solutions that accord with the evolutionary impetus that drives development in the universe. Contributing to this objective has been, and to this day it is, the motivation of my third-stage "re-reincarnation."

I am puzzled by the identities I assumed in my two previous incarnations, even in the academic incarnation. How could I dedicate the bulk of my time and energies to solving conceptual problems and finding explanations for them without recognizing that I have an urgent moral and intellectual obligation to make my work relevant to a greater and more important problem in the world?

This "closer look" at my original incarnation and subsequent reincarnations reveals what I see as the next stage of my journey. My current identity is not fixed and unalterable: It remains open to further transformations. As I approach my ninetieth year, I sense that another expansion of my identity is about to occur. It could be one in which I find myself fully and consciously devoting my life to championing the evolution of human life in the world. But I am not trying to direct this expansion; it must come on its own, I need only to remain open to embrace it. Life, after all, is an ongoing creative adventure, an unfolding of the cosmic process we call evolution.

Pursuing the Quest:
Where I Am Today

I HAVE NOW SPENT OVER SIXTY YEARS seeking to substantiate and confirm my intuitive sense that there is a purpose behind the events of my life. The question I have been asking is: What would that purpose be—the purpose of my life and of all the life in the universe? Have I found the answer to this query, or have I at least come closer to finding it? It is clear that whatever answer I may have found cannot be final and definitive. In regard to this question, as with all fundamental questions, absolute certainty is excluded. But plausible answers can be found.

Let me now ask how far I have come to finding a plausible answer to my query about the purpose of life. Here is an interim assessment.

In my recently published book *The Wisdom Principles*, I write that the key to understanding the purpose of our life is the recognition that we are not *bio-physical* but *psycho-physical* beings. On the one hand, we are bodies: matter-like vibrations in a cosmic field. But on the other hand, we are mind-like vibrations in the field—intrinsic parts of the spirit that pervades the universe:*

> Life in every person follows its own evolutionary trajectory. Through our body, we *observe* the evolution of matter-like vibrations (material bodies); and through our mind, we *experience* the evolution of mind-like vibrations (our consciousness). We *observe* that matter-like vibrations, "bodies," evolve toward higher and higher levels of coherence and complexity, and we *experience* that clusters of mind-like vibrations, consciousness, evolve (or can evolve) toward higher and higher levels of integration and coherence. The higher levels characterize the mindset of mature individuals. They embody an awareness of embracing oneness and unconditional love.
>
> The matter-like and mind-like evolutions unfold simultaneously. They are distinct but not categorically separate: they are processes in the same universe. Evolution in the universe is oriented at the same time toward higher and higher levels of complexity and coherence, and more and more embracing perception of oneness and feeling of love.
>
> But what is the purpose of these simultaneously unfolding processes? We can discover the answer to this query by noting the direction taken by these evolutions. The direction is ascension toward higher and higher levels of complexity and coherence in regard to the body,

---

* Ervin Laszlo, *The Wisdom Principles* (New York: St. Martin's Press, MacMillan Group, 2021).

and toward higher and higher levels of oneness and love in the domain of consciousness.

The purpose of life is one, but it manifests in two principal ways. One of its manifestations is the evolution of the body—the living organism. This is evolution toward higher and higher forms and levels of coherence. The other way is the evolution of consciousness. This evolution is toward higher and higher levels of oneness, and more and more profound and encompassing forms of love.

This passage from *The Wisdom Principles* gives an indication of the conclusions I reached as I tackled the problem of the purpose of life, but these conclusions need to be completed. We need to recognize that there is a higher or deeper reality beyond the phenomena we perceive with our senses. The phenomena we perceive, Plato said, are only shadows on the wall of a cave, cast by the light of a fire behind us. We do not see the source of the light, only its shadows, and we think the shadows are the reality. Recognizing a higher or deeper reality is essential to finding a meaningful answer to the question, *why am I here?*

The latest developments in the natural sciences, especially in physics and physical cosmology, provide significant indications of the existence of a deeper dimension. This is the dimension David Bohm called the "implicate order." It underlies the phenomenal "explicate order" and conveys active information to it. This information Bohm calls "in-formation" (written with a hyphen).

The world we observe is not a passive and neutral ground for the phenomena that appear in it. The universe is an active, "in-formed" domain. In this domain, not everything that is possible is equally likely to happen. Some events are more probable than others, and the distribution of their probabilities creates the phenomena that meets our eye. Although in a given situation A and B are equally possible, there is a statistically exhibited probability that B happens more often than A. Even such a subtle bias, repeated in the explicate order over myriad interactions, can create a nonrandom universe. Evolution is not a random process. Despite numerous bifurcations and temporary halts and reversals, on the whole it is directionally biased.

We can identify the "directional in-formation" that is at work in the universe: it is an active prompt, an "in-formation" that favors the emergence of dynamically stable integral ensembles of diverse elements: It is the subtle but effective impetus that creates complex and coherent systems in nature.

We find evidence for this conclusion when we take the highest level birds-eye view of evolution. We then find that in the course of time the overall state of the universe shifts from an unordered initial state toward states characterized by higher and higher forms and higher levels of complexity and coherence. Yet it is astronomically improbable that a series of random interactions would produce the complex and coherent entities that we now discover—and we ourselves exemplify.

There is directional information in the universe, an impetus that gives evolutionary processes a preferred direction. But how can we define the nature of that information?

The Abrahamic religions (at least their principal branches of Judaism, Christianity, and Islam) ascribe the source of the information that creates the world to God: a transcendental being. They assume the existence of a Creator who creates the phenomena we encounter. But is a transcendental Creator the only meaningful answer to the question regarding the nature of the directional in-formation that governs developments in the universe?" We should look at possible alternatives.

Directional in-formation is not necessarily the will of a transcendental Being. It could also be a factor that is immanent in the world, as the mystical religions of Asia and the animistic traditions of indigenous cultures maintain.

The "immanent spirit" view is not unique to Eastern religions and indigenous peoples. Surprisingly, its equivalent appears in science when the implications of current discoveries in quantum physics, quantum cosmology, and quantum biology are spelled out. The emerging realization, as I have noted in the introductory "Word to the Reader," is grounded in the fact that it is astronomically improbable that the universe we observe would have come about through chance interactions. There must be "something" more than the random play of interactions. The question is, what would that something be?

The least speculative and scientifically most acceptable answer is that this factor is immanent in the universe. It is not a transcendental will or disposition, nor an unidentified "fifth force." It is a dynamic tendency, a "bias," coming to light in the statistics of myriad interactions. The source of this subtle bias is the universe itself, but that source is not in the same dimension of the universe as the phenomena it affects.

The universe, scientists now recognize, has more than one dimension. There is a deeper dimension, as Platonists have maintained for over two and a half thousand years, and that quantum scientists are now rediscovering. The deeper dimension acts on the manifest dimension. This subtle but effective impetus is best viewed as the effect of an "attractor."

Systems scientists know that systems display elements of order that can be mapped as governed by "attractors." Given that the universe manifests a statistically significant tendency toward coherence and wholeness, we can call this attractor "holotropic"—a tendency toward creating complex and coherent wholes. These wholes are the natural systems that appear in space and time.

Leading scientists, including Einstein, Planck, Jung, and Schrödinger, did not hesitate to refer to this coherence and complexity-creating bias "as Spirit" or "Intelligence." It is equally appropriate, and less speculative in regard to its connotations, to call it an attractor— more exactly, a *holotropic* attractor.

The holotropic attractor, the same as the laws of nature, is not transcendent in the sense of being above or beyond the universe. But it is transcendent in that it originates in a deeper dimension of the universe.

The holotropic attractor "in-forms" every quantum and every system of quanta in the world, from the smallest system of molecules to the largest system of galaxies. In the language of religion and spirituality, the holotropic attractor is the divine spark in the heart of every being; and in the language of culture, it is the source of the inspiration that guides artists and other sensitive and intuitive people to think and act consistently with the rhythms and balances of nature.

The holotropic attractor has been, and continues to be, the source of my lifelong intuition that there is a purpose underlying my life, and all life on Earth and in the universe.

The View from the Mountaintop

I HAVE NOW REACHED A STAGE IN MY QUEST to understand the purpose of life where I dare to venture beyond the bounds of purely empirical reasoning to encompass the large—indeed the largest—picture. I now ask: If we ascend to the mountaintop, what view will greet our eyes? What can we say within the bounds, if not of classical science, then of the emerging quantum physics, about the nature of the world—and of human beings in the world?

1. The Widest View of the World

Let us consider the nature of the world. If the world we encounter is the product of a process of evolution, it has not always been what it is today: it has evolved into what it is. More exactly, it has evolved from an original state.

We can define the original ground-state of the cosmos with a scientific term of German origin: it is the "Ur-State." The Ur-State is the ground state of the ultimate, all-embracing totality the Greeks in turn called Kosmos. This state is constituted neither of matter nor of energy: it is a state beyond space and time, a sea of pure potentialities—an as yet undifferentiated Oneness.

After unfathomable eons of time, the Ur-State begins to differentiate. Explosive events pattern its oceanic wholeness. These events are singularities that catalyze the emergence of finite, spacetime-bounded universes. Our universe is one among these universes. It was born in the "big bang" (which was only one of a multitude of singularities or "bangs") 13.8 billion years before our time. It gave birth to the finite space-time-bounded universe we observe and inhabit.

Our universe, the same as all universes in the Kosmos, can be viewed as a pattern of waves generated by an explosive singularity. The wavefronts radiate from their point of occurrence and create complex interference patterns. Some of the patterns are constituted of waves that are in phase, and thus they have a level of stability. They persist with their own identity in the cauldron of ceaseless transformations in the early universe. The in-phase patterns do not vanish after their emergence but endure for a finite, conceivably long, span of time. These wave patterns are the entities we know as quanta: the basic units of the observable and measurable world. They create further stable or semi-stable configurations of in-phase waves: the atoms of the elements. Their interactions create still more complex interference patterns: the chemical, and then the organic molecules. The singularity that produced our spacetime universe evolves a complex and coherent substructure.

The emerging wave interference-patterns are not separate entities but integral elements of the cosmic oneness. This oneness has both a physical and a mental, psychological dimension. As a result, the universes created by a singularity are not purely physical universes; they are psychophysical universes emerging in a psychophysical Ur-State.

The stable or semi-stable patterns that emerge have themselves a physical and a psychological dimension. Their *physical* dimension is marked by the appearance, disappearance, and reappearance of variously complex and coherent wave-interference patterns, while their *psychological* dimension manifests as the localized (but intrinsically nonlocal) forms of the consciousness dimension of the Ur-State. These are the forms of consciousness we view as the consciousness "of" the patterns. Unlike the physical dimension of the patterns, this consciousness persists indefinitely in the progressively structured and differentiated Ur-State.

Universe after universe is created in the wake of local singularities. Universe after universe is born, and universe after universe vanishes at the final breakdown of the coherence of the wave patterns that constitute them. The Big Freeze of an open universe, and the Big Crunch of a closed universe, mark the end of the physical dimension of the singularity-created universes.

The physical dimension of the universes is limited in both space and time: the patterns of waves that constitute them are temporary modulations of the sea of potentials that is the cosmic Ur-State. The psychological dimension of the universes is not limited in time. Localized, but inherently nonlocal forms of consciousness evolve, become more articulate and interconnected, and remain conserved in the deeper implicate order. The evolution of the consciousness that appears to be the consciousness "of" living organisms is the outcome of the cosmic evolutionary process.

The Universe: A Whispering Pond

Come,
Sail with me on a quiet pond.
The shores are shrouded,
The surface is smooth.
We are vessels on the pond,
And we are one with the pond.

A fine wake spreads behind us,
Traveling across the misty waters.
Its subtle waves record our passage.
Your wake and mine coalesce and become one,
The pattern they form mirrors your movement and mine.

Other vessels, who are also us,
Sail the pond that is us as well;
Their wakes coalesce and become one with our wake.
The pond comes alive with ripple upon ripple,
        wave upon wave.
They are the memory of our existence;
        the record of our being.

The rippling waters whisper from you to me and
        from me to you,
And from both of us to all who sail the pond:
Our separateness is an illusion;
We are integral parts of the pond;
Together we are an evolving whole with memory.
Our reality is larger than you and me,
And all the vessels that sail the waters,
*And all the waters on which they sail.**

---

* The original version of this poem appeared in *The Emerging Vision of Science*
by Ervin Laszlo. (Rockport, Shaftesbury, Brisbane: Element Books, 1996.)

2. The Widest View of Ourselves

Despite the question's seeming simplicity, knowing who we are is one of the greatest challenges confronting the human intellect. Today we have better information at our disposal for confronting this question than ever before. We start with a natural science-based definition.

Who we are, who I am, in the physical-biological perspective of the natural sciences, is "a system of cells and organs constituting a biological organism." But the current natural science perspective needs to be expanded because this is not all who I am. I am a being with consciousness, aware of himself as well as of the world. I have a personal identity distinguishing me among the myriad beings with whom I share the planet. My consciousness makes me a unique entity in the biosphere, not because other entities would not possess consciousness, but because my consciousness, the human consciousness, is a uniquely evolved form of consciousness in this corner of the universe.

What does the possession of an evolved consciousness imply for understanding who I am—who a human being is? Alternative definitions exist. These are: (1) I am a physical-biological being who has consciousness, or (2) I am a spiritual being who has a physical-biological body. *I am a body that generates the stream of sensations we call consciousness, or a consciousness with a body that displays the sensations.* Who am I truly? Do I *have* consciousness, or *am I* consciousness?

My consciousness could be a kind of illusion, a set of sensations produced by the workings of my brain. But it could also be that my body is but a vehicle, a transmitter of the consciousness that exists above and beyond me in the world. The universe could be material, and mind an illusion. Or the universe could be consciousness, and the materiality of the world could be the illusion.

These alternatives have been explored time and time again in the history of science and spirituality. Fresh light on them is emerging at the expanding frontier where consciousness research joins natural science. On the basis of a growing series of observations, the consensus emerges that what we have classically defined as the "spiritual" alternative is the plausible one. It is likely that "my" consciousness is a real and objectively present element in the universe—it is not just *my* consciousness any more than a program transmitted over the air would be the program of my TV set or computer. My consciousness could be, and with growing assurance we can say that it most likely is, an integral part of the universe. My brain and body do not produce it; they merely display it. In the final count, "my" consciousness is a reflection, a projection, or a manifestation, of the consciousness objectively present in the world. Thus "my" consciousness is not mortal: it is an integral part of the infinite consciousness that pervades the world—and in the final count, *is* the world.

Afterword

Stanislav Grof

DURING THE SECOND HALF of the 20th century and the beginning of the 21st century many scientific observations emerged that could not be adequately explained in terms of the monistic materialistic worldview of the Newtonian-Cartesian paradigm. These "anomalous phenomena" came from astrophysics, quantum-relativistic physics, and chemistry and extended to biology, anthropology, thanatology, parapsychology, and psychology. Pioneering scientists from various fields have made more or less successful attempts to propose a radically different understanding of reality and a new paradigm in science.

In the center of the contest to create a new paradigm and map of reality has been Ervin Laszlo, the world's greatest system theorist, interdisciplinary scientist, and philosopher. It is very rare to find a more multifaceted individual with a comparable range of gifts, talents, and scientific interests. Ervin resembles one of the great figures of Renaissance. He achieved international fame as a child prodigy and in his teens performed as a concert pianist. A few years later, he turned to science and philosophy, beginning his lifetime search for the understanding of the universe, the nature of reality, and human nature.

Ervin Laszlo has been able to achieve a creative interdisciplinary synthesis of a wide range of diverse scientific fields, including astrophysics, quantum-relativistic physics, biology, parapsychology, and transpersonal psychology. He offered brilliant solutions for the "anomalous phenomena" and the baffling paradigmatic challenges for which there had been no explanation in the past. Using his unique systemic and interdisciplinary "map of everything," he was able to dissolves the boundaries between natural sciences, psychology, philosophy, and spirituality. Ken Wilber expressed in his writings the need for an integral theory of everything and outlined what such a theory should look like (*A Theory of Everything*, 2000). However, the credit for actually creating such a theory goes to Ervin Laszlo.

I would like to focus on two of the many groundbreaking contributions that Ervin's work has made. These areas are closest to my heart—consciousness research and transpersonal psychology, the field of which I have been a cofounder.

In the late 1960s, I was invited to participate in the meeting of a small group of people in Palo Alto, California. It included Abraham Maslow, Tony Sutich, Jim Fadiman, Miles Vich, Sonya Margulies, and me. We formulated the basic principles of transpersonal psychology or the "Fourth Force." This name was coined by Abe Maslow because it was the fourth major American psychology school after behaviorism, psychoanalysis, and humanistic psychology.

Transpersonal psychology explores the entire range of the human psyche, including non-ordinary states of consciousness, and it attempts to synthetize the best of spirituality and modern science. As we conceived it, transpersonal psychology is respectful of the ritual and spiritual traditions of ancient and native peoples and gives them the reverence they deserve. It also embraces and integrates a wide range of transpersonal experiences and other paradigm-breaking observations ("anomalous phenomena"). Academic circles were, and still are, unable to account for and explain these observations. Although comprehensive and well substantiated in and of itself, transpersonal psychology represented a radical departure from academic thinking.

The existence and the nature of transpersonal experiences violate some of the most basic assumptions of materialistic science. They imply such seemingly absurd notions as the relativity and arbitrary nature of physical boundaries; nonlocal connections in the universe; communication through unknown means and channels; memory without a material substrate; the nonlinearity of time, and the consciousness associated with all living organisms, even inorganic entities. Many transpersonal experiences include events from both microcosm and macrocosm, realms that cannot normally be reached unaided by human senses, as well as from historical periods that precede the origin of the solar system, the formation of planet earth, the appearance of living organisms, the development of the nervous system, and the emergence of Homo sapiens.

As a result, the new field was extremely exposed to accusations of being "irrational," "unscientific," and even "flakey." These critics, were not aware of the vast body of observations and data on which the new movement was based. They also ignored that many of the pioneers of this revolutionary movement had impressive academic credentials. They generated and embraced the transpersonal vision of the human psyche not because they were ignorant of the fundamental assumptions of traditional science, but because they found the old conceptual frameworks seriously inadequate and incapable to account for their experiences and observations.

The status of transpersonal psychology changed dramatically during the first three decades of its existence. The astonishing convergence between the worldview of modern physics and that of the Eastern spiritual philosophies, foreshadowed already in the works of Albert Einstein, Werner Heisenberg, Niels Bohr, and others, found full expression in Fritjof Capra's groundbreaking *The Tao of Physics* (1975). Important further contributions were David Bohm's explicate and implicate order, and his theory of the holomovement (1980). Bohm and his friend, the neurosurgeon Karl Pribram who created the holographic brain theory, gained great popularity in the transpersonal field. Another welcome addition to the list of works in transpersonal psychology was Rupert Sheldrake's theory of morphic resonance and morphogenetic fields. He demonstrated the importance of nonphysical fields for the understanding of forms, genetics and heredity, order, meaning, and the process of learning. Ilya Prigogine received a Nobel Prize for his study of dissipative structures and the emergence of order out of chaos in 1980; James Glieck contributed the theory of chaos in 1987, and Barrow and Tipler's anthropic principle in astrophysics was published in 1986.

All these revolutionary advances in science were welcomed in transpersonal circles as significant conceptual support for the field of transpersonal psychology. They undermined various aspects of the structure of the traditional materialistic worldview. They often brought new insights, which seemed to provide supportive evidence for various partial claims by the pioneers of the transpersonal perspective. However, what was still missing was a large integrative vision, the "conceptual glue" that would weave all these pieces into a comprehensive tapestry.

Ervin Laszlo's discoveries turned out to be the "Rosetta Stone" the pioneers of consciousness research and transpersonal psychology have been seeking. His contributions represent the quantum leap in this conceptual evolution and revolution. He reviewed the most important theories, in which various pioneers attempted to solve a number of puzzles, paradoxes, and "anomalous phenomena." He showed both the strengths and the weaknesses of the work of David Bohm, Karl Pribram, Rupert Sheldrake, Ilya Prigogine, and others and offered an elegant comprehensive metatheory that addressed unsolved problems in a number of disciplines.

My first meeting with Ervin was at the conference of the Scientific and Medical Network in Oxford. I heard Ervin's lecture

on his concept of what he then called the Psi Field and then read
his book *The Creative Cosmos*. I was excited because I heard
for the first time a plausible scientific explanation of the fantastic experiences recounted by my clients in their LSD sessions, and in sessions of my own. One of the most astonishing
observations in psychedelic and holotropic breathwork sessions
is the possibility of time travel to different historical periods
and countries. I have in my records many reports of individuals who were convinced that they experienced events that took
place in ancient Assyria or Babylonia, in Japan at the time of the
samurais, in the French Revolution, in colonial Africa, and in
many other places and times.

Ancestral, racial, collective, and past incarnation experiences frequently provide very specific details about architec-
ture, costumes, weapons, art forms, social structure, and the
religious or ritual practices of a given culture and historical
period, even sometimes providing specific historical events. I
have personally experienced what appear to be convincing past
life experiences in ancient Egypt and Czarist Russia and experienced similar sequences from ancient and more recent historical periods in various geographical locations.

Professionals who had these experiences in their psychedelic
sessions—for example, Tim Leary—tried to find a materialistic
substrate for these experiences; they thought that it was possible to receive this information from DNA. But they realized
that the "psychonauts" often experientially identified themselves with persons from different racial groups; for example,

a Slavic person identified himself with a Japanese samurai, an Anglo-Saxon with a black African slave, and a Chinese with a Spanish conquistador.

Transpersonal experiences often include authentic experiential identification with animals. Ervin's new map of reality makes this possible as it expanded from the physically centered Psi Field to the Akashic Holofield. The validation of the received information is often easier in animals than in humans. Many important aspects of the animals that we experience in psychedelic sessions cannot be conveyed by the conventional media of books, photographs, movies, or videos. These media can only portray what these animals look like and what sounds they make.

In transpersonal experiences we can assume the body image of these animals and know their proprioceptive sensations: what they feel, smell, or taste. My friend John Lilly, the neurophysiologist dedicated to exploring dolphin intelligence, took LSD and experienced identification with the dolphins. He described for me what their world looked like. According to him, the dolphins rely on acoustic input and create their world primarily by the sonar rather than optical stimuli. Transpersonal experiences concerning animals sometimes also offer extraordinary insights on animal psychology, ethology, courtship dances, and mating habits.

These observations indicate that we can obtain information about the universe in two radically different ways. Besides the conventional possibility of learning through sensory perception and the analysis and synthesis of the data, we can also discover various aspects of the world by direct identification with them in a holotropic state of consciousness. Each of us thus seems to be a microcosm that has access to information on the macrocosm.

For over six decades, Ervin's remarkable tour de force of multidisciplinary research, discoveries, and concepts have been illuminating most of the questions and riddles that have vexed transpersonal psychologists. The most important overall conclusion we can draw from his and other avenues of modern consciousness research is that consciousness is not a product of the neurophysiological processes in the brain. It is an essentially cosmic phenomenon, an integral part of existence in the universe. This realization is the basic tenet of Laszlo's map of reality. According to him, consciousness does not originate in the brain; it originates beyond spacetime in the domain of the Akashic Holofield. The "in-formation" in this realms forms and in-forms all entities and phenomena in spacetime. The spacetime domain contains the information and the rules and regularities that govern behavior in the manifest world. It conserves a complete holographic record of the history of the universe and our planet, including the patterns of consciousness it has created. Since this domain has no boundaries and partitions, all the in-formation contained in it is present in all its points as in a hologram.

Many problems related to transpersonal experiences can be resolved if we accept Laszlo's postulate of the Akashic Holofield. These include experiences from the past such as Jung's synchronicities, extrasensory perceptions, out-of-body-experiences, near-death experiences, astral projections, and experiential identification with other people, animals, and plants—among many others.

Ervin Laszlo is one of the greatest scientists and philosophers of our time. He has published more than 100 books and over 400 articles and research papers. He is recipient of various honors and awards, including honorary PhDs from several countries. He is the founder and president of the international think tank The Club of Budapest and of the prestigious Laszlo Institute of New Paradigm Research and was twice nominated for the Nobel Peace Prize. I believe that in the future Ervin's extraordinary intellectual achievements will be seen as marking a critical turning point in the history of science, and very likely as the foundation of the twenty first century's new scientific paradigm.

ANNEX
Expanding the Quest

FOURTEEN THOUGHT LEADERS COMMENT ON WHY WE ARE HERE

This annex expands the scope of the quest for the purpose of life. Ours is not a randomly emerging universe, and there is a reason why and how life emerges on Earth and wherever physical conditions permit.

As already discussed, scientific findings affirm that the universe is not random even if it manifests chaotic elements and temporary halts and reversals. The universe is an integral whole moving inexorably toward higher and higher states and higher and higher levels of coherence and complexity. It is the way it is because there is an intrinsic impetus driving it, a wholeness-oriented tropism. This impetus is likely to be in every being that evolves and persists in space and time.

Humanity is part of the universe, and it follows that whatever impetus drives the universe toward complexity and coherence is present in every human being. When insightful people ask themselves "Why are we here?" and dare to speculate on the answer, this impetus finds expression.

For the purpose of this book, fourteen eminent scientists and thought leaders have been invited to ask themselves this question. Their answers are recorded on the pages that follow.

Allan Leslie Combs

T he purpose and meaning of life is presented here in the form of many voices:

- ✧ *The present writer speaking in the 3rd person*
- ✧ *The present writer revealing an inner voice*
- ✧ *Ervin Laszlo's voice in this book*
- ✧ *The voices of selected writers*

"The journey of my life is the story of the pursuit of a quest. It is a basic quest, simple in conception, but challenging in practice. It is no less than to find the purpose of my life. I can say 'my life' without being egocentric and blind to others because I am convinced that the purpose that underlies my life is the purpose that underlies all life on the planet, and indeed all life that is likely to emerge in the wide reaches of the universe. The consciousness of this purpose, and the attempt to live up to it, endows my life with meaning."

—Ervin Laszlo
(paraphrased from this book)

The cosmos presents itself to us as a grand stream, flowing onward toward increasing complexity, coherence, and unity. The human is a fish, carried forward in this great stream, embodying an evolutionary mandate to seek increasing complexity, coherence, and unity.

Each human life follows this basic pattern, starting from Sophocles' four-legged creature, the human infant, whose nascent purpose is limited to nursing and sleeping, soon to be followed by toilet training and learning to avoid punishment. Then comes early childhood, during which avoiding punishment is gradually replaced by seeking pleasure. Here I live in the moment, and have no sense of myself. My actions are purposeful, but unconscious. For me, the world exists as I see it through my eyes and hear it though my ears.

> "When we are children we seldom think of the future. This innocence leaves us free to enjoy ourselves as few adults can. The day we fret about the future is the day we leave our childhood behind."
>
> —PATRICK ROTHFUSS
> *The Name of the Wind*

I become a two-legged creature and remain so for many years, growing through childhood, and developing a first budding sense of who I really am, where I live, who I live with, and who I depend on for nourishment and safety.

Coming into late childhood, my intelligence and understanding of the wide world around me matures palpably. In many ways I now feel I am an adult. Internally, though, my sense of right and wrong, and how I see others, is limited to fact-like rules learned at home or at school. I understand that others are often sad or in pain, but I have no direct understanding of their experience. I am told that others see the world differently than I, but I understand this only in the most literal way. I have no clue as to what it is like to be and experience life as another living being.

Well, along in childhood I wake up. This is an example of how that works:

> "She had been playing houses in a nook right in the bows . . . thinking vaguely about some bees and a fairy queen, when it suddenly flashed into her mind that she was *she*."
>
> "She stopped dead, and began looking over all of her person which came within the range of her eyes. She could not see much, except a foreshortened view of the front of her frock, and her hands when she lifted them for inspection; but it was enough for her to form a rough idea of the little body she suddenly realized to be *hers*."
>
> "She began to laugh, rather mockingly. " Well!" she thought, in effect. "Fancy you, of all people, going and getting caught like this! You can't get out of it now, not for a very long time: you'll have to go through with being a child, and growing up, and getting old, before you' ll be quit of this mad prank!"
>
> —RICHARD HUGHES in his 1928 book,
> *A High Wind in Jamaica: The Innocent Voyage.*

Waking up made a big difference in how I see myself and my life in the world.

Adolescence

"My father did not share my uncle's philosophical concerns, and my mother was too concentrated on music to enter into them. My uncle had me, an early teenager, as his avid listener. Our afternoon walks in the city park across from our house made a deep impression, although I did not realize it until much later. I was not inclined to accept any preconceived idea without further scrutiny, and my uncle's ideas rather than being taken over by me, catalyzed the steps that have then led to the clarification of my own ideas. Even if they needed clarification subsequently, *my ideas have always come to me on their own, seemingly out of the blue.*"

—ERVIN LASZLO (from this book)

As I grow into my adolescent years, the purpose of my life changes from having fun while avoiding emotional and physical discomfort into fitting in socially with other young people my age, seeking their acceptance and approval, and participating in their activities, such as games, sports, and social events.

I seem to spend a lot of time trying to figure out who I am.

"Standing in the line at the food court, I try to be myself. But I forget how I usually stand when I'm myself."

—SUSANE COLASANTI
"When It Happens," 2008

Adolescent life can be frustrating.

"So you try to think of someone else you're mad at, and the unavoidable answer pops into your little warped brain: everyone."

—ELLEN HOPKINS
Impulse

Early Adulthood

Growing into young adulthood, my world is increasingly about the great projects of achieving professional success and of parenting my own children. I am taking a logical and determined approach to these, and working diligently for their success.

It seems Ervin got an early start on growing up through his musical performances.

"I became known as a "piano prodigy." My formal debut was with the Budapest Philharmonic at the age of nine, performing the Mozart Piano Concerto in A major. Other appearances followed, both in recitals and as soloist with symphony orchestras."

—ERVIN LASZLO (2021)

Adult life is purposeful and satisfactory. But . . .

"The seeds sown by my conversations with my philosopher uncle were dormant, but not lost. In my late teens and early twenties they returned to influence my thinking and my whole view of the world. My life took an unusual and

unexpected turn: it began to transform into a different
mold . . . I seemed impelled to question and rethink."

—Ervin Laszlo (from this book)

Midlife

Eventually I tire and begin to lose interest in my professional
life, and my mind begins wander toward other more meaningful explorations.

"A resolution took form in my mind that turned out to be
not just a new-year's but a new life's resolution. For years,
I had a profound sense that my life has a purpose, and
that I should be living by that purpose. What is the life
purpose of a concert pianist? To be the best pianist he/
she could possibly be? Or was it something else as well?
I had a definite feeling that there is more to fulfilling the
purpose of my life than achieving success on the concert
stage. Was the purpose of my life to experience perfection—in music, but not only in music?"

—Ervin Laszlo (from this book)

"The commonsense way to follow up my new-year's (or
new-life's) resolution would have been to take science
and philosophy courses at a university . . . But I postponed enrolling until later. First, I wanted to reach down
and understand my experience on my own. I had an
intuitive sense that the answer is in me, if only I could
uncover it."

—Ervin Laszlo (from this book)

"Healthy introspection, without undermining oneself; it is a rare gift to venture into the unexplored depths of the self, without delusions or fictions, but with an uncorrupted gaze."

—FRIEDRICH NIETZSCHE
Unpublished Writings from the Period of
Unfashionable Observations
from *The Complete Works of Friedrich Nietzsche*

This can be an unsettling adventure. The emerging existential mind reaches out for new and deeper answers. Ervin seems to have made it through safely, and then pushed on.

"You don't have to stay anywhere forever."

—NEIL GAIMAN
The Kindly Ones

"To live on a day-to-day basis is insufficient for human beings; we need to transcend, transport, escape; we need meaning, understanding, and explanation; we need to see over-all patterns in our lives."

—OLIVER SACKS
"Altered States: Self-Experiments in Chemistry,"
The New Yorker, 2012

Thoughts Leads to Activism

"I left the U.N. and retired to our family retreat in the hills of Tuscany. This was to be a year of repose and renewal, taking a fresh breath and turning over a new leaf. But that "sabbatical year," starting in 1984, did not end after a year—it did not end to this day. It proved to be a period of active and intense work: activism in the interest of creating a better world."

—ERVIN LASZLO (from this book)

"How wonderful it is that nobody need wait a single moment before starting to improve the world."

—ANNE FRANK
Anne Frank's Diary of a Young Girl

"Never doubt that a small group of thoughtful, committed, citizens can change the world. Indeed, it is the only thing that ever has."

—Often attributed to MARGARET MEAD,
but actual source is unknown

"Unless someone like you cares a whole awful lot,
Nothing is going to get better. It's not."

—DR. SEUSS
The Lorax

Awakening Into the Future

The randomness-reducing subtle but effective impetus in the universe, I conclude, is not a Being, and not a Force. It is the immanent variety of what the religions call Mind or Spirit. The

Cosmic Consciousness "in-forms" the interactions that take place in space and time . . . In the language of systems science, it is a subtle but effective attractor that biases interactions in a definite direction. In the language of religion, in turn, it is a divine spark present in every entity in the world . . .

"An awake heart is like a sky that pours light."

—Attributed to Sufi poet HAFI

"You have no choice. You must leave your ego
on the doorstep before you enter love."

—Attributed to KAMAND KOJOURI

"To recognize one's own insanity is, of course, the arising
of sanity, the beginning of healing and transcendence."

—ECKHART TOLLE
A New Earth

"Who would then deny that when I am sipping tea in my tea room I am swallowing the whole universe with it and that this very moment of my lifting the bowl to my lips is eternity itself transcending time and space?"

—Attributed to DAISETZ TEITARO SUZUKI

"Might we begin then to transform our passing illuminations into abiding light?"

—Attributed to HUSTON SMITH,
author of *The World's Religions*

"We are all butterflies. Earth is our chrysalis."

—LeeAnn Taylor
The Fragile Face of God: A True Story About Light,
Darkness, and the Hope Beyond the Veil

"In the point of rest at the center of our being, we encounter a world where all things are at rest in the same way. Then a tree becomes a mystery, a cloud a revelation, each man a cosmos of whose riches we can only catch glimpses. The life of simplicity is simple, but it opens to us a book in which we never get beyond the first syllable."

—Dag Hammarskjöld
Markings

"Not known, because not looked for
But heard, half-heard, in the stillness
Between two waves of the sea.
Quick now, here, now, always—
A condition of complete simplicity
(Costing not less than everything)
And all shall be well and
All manner of thing shall be well
When the tongues of flames are in-folded
Into the crowned knot of fire
And the fire and the rose are one."

—"The Little Gidding,"
T. S. Eliot: *Four Quartets*

"The great use of life is to spend it for something that outlasts it."

—WILLIAM JAMES
From the book *The Thought and Character of William: As Revealed in Unpublished Correspondence and Notes, Together with his Published Writings,* 1935

"I cannot believe that the purpose of life is to be "happy." I think the purpose of life is to be useful, to be responsible, to be honorable, to be compassionate. It is above all, to matter: to count, to stand for something, to have made some difference that you lived at all."

—LEON C. RESTON, quoted in
Words of Wisdom: More Good Advice,
Compiled and edited by William Safire and Leonard Safire, 1989

JUDE CURRIVAN

Ervin was already an internationally celebrated concert pianist while I was growing up in a coal mining family in the north of England in the "swinging 60s." Along with most of my friends, my musical heroes were the pop idols of that time, led of course by the Beatles. Other influences were my beloved mum's delight in musicals, my uncle's love of opera, our communal singing of hymns and especially carols at Christmas, and occasional access to the inspiration of classical music. Through such eclectic influences, I deeply felt the power of music, and would regularly embarrass myself by it bringing me to tears.

My own musical expertise was recognized by my being relegated to playing the triangle in the percussion section of my high school orchestra. With such modest skills, I've always held in awe those, such as Ervin, who are gifted with the ability that I realize also entails great commitment and embodied inspiration, to be musicians of the highest caliber and genius.

Rather like Ervin, though, I never queried whether music has a purpose, I just knew it does.

Being recognized as a musical prodigy from a young age, Ervin was rightly feted. In my own case, as a small child, already hugely curious about the nature of the world and not fitting in very well with my surroundings, I was, as many others before and since, was merely considered odd. Unbeknownst to virtually everyone, except mum, who patiently answered my never-ending questions of "why," I'd begun a lifelong journey of exploration and discovery. Even she, though she was unaware of just how far I was already traveling and to what extent I was hearing and listening to the ancient philosophers' perception of the "music of the spheres."

From the age of four, I was directly experiencing multidimensional realities and phenomena, such as remote viewing and precognition. These were simply "supernormal" for me. Also, as a voracious reader, seeking further help to explain both the why and how of my experiences, I was intuitively drawn to ancient and indigenous wisdom teachings, and intellectually to scientific theories and the evidence. I discovered that the wisdom teachings offered many satisfying and in-depth insights. Mainstream science however, provided a predominantly mechanistic view of what I was increasingly aware was only the appearance of the universe and not its deeper reality, meaning, and purpose.

Ervin's quest to understand the nature of reality and the meaningful purpose of existence, called him far beyond his love of music. Like the excellent scientist he also is, his determination to follow the evidence, wherever it led, is one I share on my own path and have always sought to do.

In the last few years, evidence at all scales of existence and across numerous and wide-ranging fields of research has revealed a holistic scientific perspective that's not only converging but integrating with universal spirituality and the ancient and indigenous wisdom teachings of many traditions. Fundamentally, it shows that mind and consciousness are not something we have, but what we and the whole world are.

While clues to this awareness are found in quantum and relativistic physics, which respectively describe energy-matter and space-time, this new perspective goes much further. It is discovering that the appearance of our universe in its totality is an emergent phenomenon of fundamental nonphysical and causative realms of cosmic intelligence. Increasing understanding of its multidimensional and unified reality is perceiving the intrinsic role of information and the so-called holographic principle, enabling us to develop its cosmological framework— essentially a cosmic hologram.

Ever increasing evidence is showing how cosmic mind, articulated as digitized and crucially meaningful information and holographically manifested in dynamic and relational patterns and processes, literally "in-forms" the reality of our universe. Its mathematical signatures are universal throughout the "natural" world and are revealed in collective human behaviors. Their self-similar fractal patterns occur at all scales of existence, from individual atoms to vast galactic clusters, to the relic radiation that fills all of space. Ecosystems embody the same patterning as does the internet, and earthquakes and human conflicts follow the same so-called power-law of how their frequencies and destructive magnitudes relate.

Discoveries are also showing that our universe was exquisitely ordered and fine-tuned from its beginning, not as the implied chaos of a big bang but the first moment of an ongoing big breath. Indeed, we know now that in its earliest epoch a primordial Aum resonated throughout space, pulsing the first energy and matter into structure. Its inherent coherence and resonance continue to embody an evolutionary impulse from simplicity to complexity and ever greater self-awareness. It meaningfully and purposefully exists in order to evolve. As its microcosmic co-creators, we are part of its evolutionary impulse and share a vital role, opportunity and choice at this pivotal moment for ourselves and for Gaia, our planetary home.

By revealing the illusion of separation, this integral whole-world view aligns with Ervin's and ever more global calls for radical change; inviting and empowering us to link up and lift up together to embody unity in diversity and co-creatively transform our world.

In viewing the existence and every differentiated and diverse aspect of the unified reality of our universe as innately meaningful and purposeful, we can experience the extraordinary in the ordinary and the ordinary in the extraordinary. We can each attune the unique notes of "me," with the collective music of "we," to sing into being the universal (r)evolutionary impulse through humanity and embody its wonder-full potential and realities within ourselves and the new song-lines of Gaia.

Ervin and I have walked different paths, as have all the contributors to this book and indeed every human being. Yet, it seems that we are all on the same journey. I wonder whether, as for Ervin, all of our routes have been guided by a quest for meaning and purpose. And perhaps, as the great Irish mystic John O'Donohue put it, we are all on a universal journey from such longing to homecomings of belonging; coming home to ourselves, to each other, to our planetary home, and to the entire Kosmos.

Amit Goswami

Ever since Isaac Newton gave us the equation of motion for material objects that shows the movement to be entirely driven by cause, the idea of cause being the only driver of movement and change has been gaining much force. To this end, Darwin's theory of evolution was interpreted in causal terms with the need for survival being the cause that drives life's evolution. More recently, neuroscientists and psychologists likewise have been prone to propagate the belief that human experience and behavior is also cause driven.

Of course, not all biologists, indeed Darwin himself, agree with this assessment. The empirically observed biological arrow of time speaks in favor of purpose. In psychology, the psychologist Abraham Maslow has theorized that humans respond to a hierarchy of needs. Whereas the lower need—survival—can be interpreted as a cause (although it is a stretch!), the higher needs such as love irrefutably smacks of purpose. And of course, many humans (witness the author of this book, Ervin Laszlo, and his contributors) believe that living beings respond to both cause and purpose; for many humans such as us, the writers of the essays in this book, purpose has played a crucial role in shaping the changes of life.

In biology, Lamarck's purposive theory of evolution has gotten a boost from the idea that evolution and development are simultaneous processes and that whereas genetic changes are causal, development involves a process of the software of living beings, and that is purposive. The discovery of the biologist Rupert Sheldrake that living software requires nonphysical morphogenetic fields for its development, and the empirical support for Sheldrake's theory that indeed living software is epigenetic, has revived the importance of purpose in biology.

Of course, spiritual teachers and religions have always promulgated the importance of meaning and purpose in human lives. Following the lead of Sri Aurobindo and Teilhard de Chardin, based on new developments of quantum physics, I have very recently developed an extension of Darwin's theory of creative evolution integrating Lamarck's and Sheldrake's ideas with Darwin's theory. That explains the fossil gaps of Darwin's original theory as well as the biological arrow of time and many other unexplained data. (I am referring to my book *Creative Evolution*, and to my upcoming *Quantum Biology* and the *Ascent of Humanity*.)

The new developments of quantum physics refer to a solution of the famous quantum measurement problem I published in a paper in 1989 and elaborated in details in the book *The Self-Aware Universe*. The solution, since verified by experimental neuroscience data, posits that consciousness is the ground of being and that quantum objects (material as well as nonmaterial) are possibilities for consciousness to choose from;

when consciousness chooses, it identifies with the brain of the observer, so that the brain and the object under observation actualizes. In this way, there is a subject-object split in the observer's experience of the world, "I see the world."

For the sake of brevity, let me cut to the chase. For producing the forgetfulness of our origin in the oneness of the ground of our being, the self that manifests in the brain operates in two modes: the mode of a conditioned ego (local) and that of a quantum self (nonlocal). The local mode is causal, but the nonlocal mode is purposive. In this way when via openness we make room in our lives for the quantum self, we open up to purpose. This is when we are capable of responding to, and exploring, higher needs through creativity.

Thus in this way the higher meanings and noble feelings are the results of the conjoined role played by both cause and purpose. Cause comes to us through sensory signals, while purpose comes through nonlocal signal-less communication from consciousness in the form of archetypes—aspects of consciousness such as love, beauty, justice, truth, wholeness, and the like.

On Ervin Laszlo

Please note how beautifully this theory fits with Ervin Laszlo's life. The first phase of his life as a piano virtuoso is a purposive pursuit of the archetype of beauty, for which he was born from past incarnations. (Yes, talent comes to us from past lives, quantum science gives us a theory of reincarnation [see my *Physics of the Soul*, Mumbai, 2018]). Subsequently, he became the explorer of the archetype of truth—and what an exploration that has been! Without going into detail, suffice it to say that he foresaw the development of quantum measurement theory and intuited that quantum collapse from possibility to actuality is an action in a quantum field that is nonlocal and therefore nonmaterial. His concept of the quantum field is what I regard as nonlocal consciousness.

In the third phase of his life, he opened up his life to purpose in the movement of consciousness itself, tirelessly propagating the importance of a new post-materialist purposive thinking.

Reflections on My Own Life

The heterogeneity of human life is no doubt partly circumstantial. Conditioned human life, if influenced by the same culture, would have otherwise been more or less homogeneous. But for some of us, life showed up with irreducible heterogeneity from the beginning, and this is due to the play of purpose.

There have been three phases in my life as well. From my past life, I brought intention and the required propensities for the exploration of the archetype of truth, which is what I admittedly initially did in a kind of partially circumstantial ho-hum way, driven more by cause than by purpose. In 1973, at the age of 37, I had a "crystallization" experience that revealed my new life's purpose—Wholeness. I was at a physics conference giving a lecture, but as I listened to others, the whole day I felt jealous and insecure. This continued through the evening at a party (when the tint of jealousy shifted to not having enough female attention!). At 1:00 a.m. I was thoroughly disgusted with myself, so I went outside to the ocean beach where a cool breeze welcomed me, and the thought came, "Why do I live this way?" It was followed by the amazing intuition, "I don't have to: I can integrate the way I think, the way I live, and the way I make my living."

That conviction became subsequently an exploration of wholeness involving the integrative exploration of the archetypes of truth and love, as well as the integration of all the dichotomies that beset human life and prevent wholeness. This I believe made all the difference in my being able to develop an integration of science and spirituality as a complete science of consciousness (*The Quantum Brain*, by Goswami and Onisor).

To end this article, I should note that at the third phase of my life I, too, like Ervin, have become a quantum activist with the objective of helping people to explore life with meaning and purpose and fulfill our human potential. To this end, I have founded an institute of purposive transformational education that awards degrees in the quantum science of health, prosperity, and happiness.

Jean Houston

Oh Ervin,

When I consider your life and work and the Spirit that informs you, I ask from what Cosmic Garden of Eden did you emerge? And toward what destiny are you pointed? Perhaps now, as the ground of the known shifts beneath our feet, what we need to steady ourselves is nothing short of a new origin-myth, an evolutionary tale such as you have been propounding, that takes your visionary science as its given, and places in perspective the suchness of your deepest personal reality:

A Meditation on the Metaverse for Ervin Laszlo

In the beginning there were and continue to be the Great Gardeners who live in the Metaverse, a vast farm fertile with energy, creativity, intelligence, and love. The Gardeners decide to plant a new garden in a field of the farm's limitless, nested universes. They begin with an infinitesimally tiny seed, a microcosm coded with the energy resources to flower into a richly varied cosmos. So potent is the ground, so ready is the seed, that once planted, it bursts its pod with an explosion of light and energy.

And lo, the infinitesimal seed sprouts into a great tree that holds in its branches a trillion galaxies, each blossoming with a hundred billion or more stars. Whirlwinds of energy swirling through the branches coalesce into biosystems of planetary scale, each home to billions of organisms that balance each other in self-sustaining ecological webs. Nourishing each bud of this immense flowering is the great tree, which links every expression of the garden's unfolding in energetic resonance, such that anything that happens in any part is known instantaneously to the whole.

As the budding life forms of the biospheres complexify, the most advanced among them jump first into awareness of themselves and then into awareness of the Great Gardeners who planted them. Problems that arise at each stage of their growth create opportunities for learning, experimentation, and new expression leading the advancing ones to deeper and more profound understanding of themselves and their world. As this understanding grows, they develop ways to meet their physical needs with less and less expenditure of energy and resources, so that more and more of their awareness can be devoted to tending the garden of their consciousness and culture. Soon the winds of the technology they have evolved are cross-pollinating the flowers of many places and knowings.

Venturing out to explore the worlds of the very large and the very small, first in their imaginations and then through their technological advances, these adventurous ones come to discover the wonders of the cosmic tree. They begin to understand that all life is engaged in a process of continuous creation and that birth, growth, death, and new birth are all expressions of energy in motion. They come to see that **the** cosmos both within and without is a living organism, a single unified garden, recreated in its entirety moment by moment by the love and intelligence of the Gardeners flowing continuously through the Great Tree like nourishing sap.

They discover, further, that along with the knowledge of the Great Tree comes a radical freedom. They know themselves to be free to make mistakes, to face evil, and to experience suffering, for suffering is the inevitable consequence of the great potential of their seeded nature, locked into a still maturing consciousness. Yet, over time, as their scope of vision widens, these beings evolve toward transcending their suffering. As they do, they come to a more and more expansive understanding of who they are and what they yet may be and do. And this brings the story up to who and what you are in this radical moment of cosmic earth history.

Knowing at last that all is within all, the totality present in each part and each part fully connected to the whole, you move beyond the limited conceptions of the local laws of form and gain access to the very patterns of creation. With this knowledge, you, my dear friend, join the Gardeners in their task of planning and planting cosmic gardens and nourishing them with their own intelligence and love. And so, the cosmos continues to bloom.

This cosmic evolutionary tale is itself a hologram for living in this critical time. It reminds us that I, and you in your own unique way, are Gardeners who can farm the fields of space/time, the generative ground of our being, creating gardens of consciousness, landscapes filled with the blossoms of our minds and spirits. Tending the gardens of your life, dear Ervin, involves a kind of cosmic yoga; you yoke yourself back to remembering that you are made of the same stuff as the Metaverse from which you continuously arise. You share its body, albeit as a manifestation of the Divine Spark in the world; you are woven into the fabric of its infinite ecology; the productions of your hands and mind—even in the crucible of crisis, are an aspect of its creation and live in eternity. You know yourself, then, as resonant waves of the original seed, an infinite being who contains in your body-mind the design of creation itself, planted in the field of this particular space-time and sustained by a dynamic flow-through of cosmic energy and the love and nurturance of the Divine Spark.

At your core, Ervin, you already know this to be so. From your reflections and meditations and your many books you understand yourself to be a reality surfer, delightedly riding the waves of creation, mind opened, heart expanded, the Metaverse coursing through you. In this state you are embraced in co-conscious awareness, no longer knowing or caring where "I" leave off and the rest of reality begins, or whether there is any difference. This experience is one of the supreme givens of our nature because the Metaverse in its operational mode is coded into every one of us, but especially in you. The raptures of the deep self are our native equipment, granted you and to me by our cosmic origins. The only requirement is joy and a willingness to say "yes" to the new epic that dawns, right now, in you and me and those fortunate to be alive in the great today. We are seeds coded with cosmic dreams. Bursting the pods of your containment you, Ervin, have led the way to entering into creative partnership with the Metaverse, and to populate our particular corner of space-time with your unique vision and capacity.

Riccardo Illy

The first aspect of Ervin Laszlo's life that thrilled me is that he is probably the sole person who did something (and did very well indeed), and then learned how to do it (and do it perhaps even better). Ervin played the piano intuitively and, still as a boy, could teach his mother how to do it; he then studied and became a star pianist. Later he felt to be "called" by more important commitments and started writing on philosophy. Only later, after he expressed and fixed his philosophical approach, did he decide to study the principal classical philosophers and to confront their views with the most important contemporary thinkers. Such a unique path could only bring a unique result—to answer the most intriguing and difficult question that, at least on the earth, only humans can ask. What is the purpose of our life?

In my life, I also had a similar experience; when I was a boy I flew with my father and the instructor in the airplane he rented to learn flying and get a license. More than ten year later, being a newly married young man, I bought a hang glider, and without any verbal or written instructions, I just flew. Remembering what the instructor said to my father, what I had to do was simply intuitive. Only some years later I decided to buy a paraglider and get the license needed at that time. I took some lessons to improve my flying skills. Although this was nothing compared to playing the piano and producing philosophical theories . . .

I, too, often asked myself, and talked with my wife, about the purpose of our life. My answer was to contribute to improving the quality of life of people. Reading the history of Ervin Laszlo's journey, many of these thoughts came again to my mind. We as human beings are animals with some additional hallmarks: We are conscious of existing, we have a distinct creativity, and we can transfer our ideas and knowledge to others. These features allowed us to know more, and to explore more of the universe. They and oblige us to try to understand the mystery of life and of death. We have some limits; we tend to think we are the sole beings in the universe who are conscious, able to think, and to create. Once we thought that other beings were living on Mars, but now this belief is gone. We think we are able to perceive and to know everything around us. There is probably much more in the universe than we can detect with our eyes, ears, mouth, nose, skin or, as in the case of electromagnetic waves, with our instruments. We tend to apply to other, still greater entities the limits of our life. For we who are human beings the concepts of infinity and of eternity are uncomfortable. As our space and time are limited, we tend to apply the same limits to the things that surround us. When speaking with concern about infinity, we only think about "wider" dimensions. But if time is eternal on two dimensions (past and future) also infinite space should be conceived in two dimensions: the larger and the smaller. In the dimensions of eternal time and infinite time we live just in the time and dimension in which we are.

To overcome the fear of death, we tend to believe that our soul will continue to exist after our body. This suggests that our soul was born with our body, but will never die. When studying the universe, we apply this same model; the universe must have been "born" one day and will live eternally. The "big bang" theory supports this assumption. I am not saying that the physics of an expanding universe are wrong. Perhaps after a phase of expansion a phase of contraction will follow. In any case it is more logical to maintain that the universe has always existed and will always exist (in a straight line) and that our soul exists only as long as our body is alive (that is a segment).

The followers of monotheistic religions tend to reinforce our expectations. Jesus is said in the Bible to have been born some 2,000 years ago, but he has never (really) died. His life is a metaphor of the life we wish to have, especially of our after-life.

Toward the end of his journey Ervin Laszlo has found the meaning of life through his philosophy. It can be summarized as seeking two states of being: coherence and oneness. It is interesting to observe that through different approaches, leading people in philosophy, science, and religion arrived at similar conclusions. And there are questions; the main question, which is already resolved by religion: A God, if it exists, is a "factor" that accounts for the organization and evolution of the universe. Ervin Laszlo calls this factor "the holotropic attractor," a merger between a psychological and a mathematical concept. The attractor impels all things toward wholeness, a subtle solution to one of the mysteries of life.

We cannot agree that everything we can perceive, from protons and electrons to the universe, developed and continues to evolve entirely spontaneously. Stuart Kauffman suggested the theory of self-organization as an account of evolution; we can also observe it in animals and human social organization. Life has the capability to change its level of entropy, fighting the natural trend toward increasing entropy. Entropy can be interpreted as the third dimension we apply when we interpret existence beyond space and time.

The two questions that Ervin raises and answers are intertwined. Only humans can ask them, and only a higher organizer, a "deeper factor," could create such a unique being. The Christian religions solved this conundrum; the son of God, Jesus, was the being in charge of representing his father on Earth. His mission was to spread the value of love. Humans feel they are one with God, having the task of disseminating His message. In Kauffman's theory, the deeper factor is self-organization. In that case humans can be interpreted as the highest level of self-organizational evolution, at least on the Earth. Then the purpose of life is something each human being can decide for his or her own life, and provided his or her purpose contains love, he or she can decide it for the better. The life of such an individual will improve the life of other people and will contribute to the conscious evolution of our species.

EMANUEL KUNTZELMAN

We express ourselves through the lens of a vast array of cultures and their languages throughout the world. No matter how we say it, the message is the same. At the core of our existence and as the goal of our journey through life, there is one, underlying and burning question that drives the decisions we make and the paths we take: What is the purpose and meaning of our life? I am sure there is a way to express it in every language. In French, it would be "raison d'être," in Japanese "ikigai." In English it is meaning and, above all, purpose.

Profound and compelling as the quest for purpose is, it is surprising that so many people abandon the search before they ever get fully started. This is because the socialization processes of human society are extremely powerful and exert pressure on us from the moment we start thinking we must toe the line to conform to the expectations of our family, teachers, and friends. The cultural conditioning we are subjected to often overrides the spirit of our individual will at an early age and, for most of us, inhibits our inner instinct to find our own personal path to purpose, especially when it does not coincide with the expectations of our social environment.

This cultural pressure to conform arose for a good reason: our survival. In the early days of humanity's quest for consciousness, the main concern was to stay alive while there were wild animals and enemy tribes lurking in the forest hoping to take our lives and possessions. Over time, this survival instinct became ingrained in our cultures to the extent that there were serious retributions for straying from the norms.

Now, in the 21st century, survival has given way to material accumulation as our number one concern, but the cultural conditioning remains as strong as ever: It implores us not to aspire to do something different, nor to find our own, creative way to success. The resounding message we hear is to be practical, get a good job, make money, raise a family, accumulate wealth, and propagate the species.

The biggest challenge we all face in life is to overcome this socialization process and believe in ourselves and our innate abilities. It is often assumed that genius is comprised of a special talent that most mere mortals will never have because they were not born with any sublime attributes of genius. That is an erroneous assumption. The doorway to genius is opened by a trait we all possess, if only we would exercise it: the will to resist cultural conditioning and allow ourselves to become the person we were meant to be.

For all his genius as a concert pianist, a writer and philosopher, and a humanitarian activist, Ervin Laszlo's greatest example to me has always been his ability—his will—to be of his own mind and do what he needed to do in order to best serve humanity. How many people who have achieved worldwide fame and renown in a given profession, such as a pianist, will dare to shift course and undertake a complex new field of endeavor at a key moment in their career? Ervin Laszlo is one of the very few who have done so, and that is the source of his genius. He understands that the quest for purpose is organic and evolutionary. Our sense of personal purpose grows faster than we do—it is always out in front of us, luring us towards the next phase of unknown mystery that our life would love to reveal to us. And Ervin heeded the call.

Extraordinary as Ervin Laszlo's personal history is, I find his account a universally "likely story" of reality. Purpose is like a seed. It settles into the world by landing somewhere on the soil, but if there isn't enough water and light, it may never grow. Unfortunately, the seeds of purpose linger in the soil of so many souls, just waiting to be watered, but never sprouting. Ervin, however, provided his own nourishment to purpose as naturally as the sun shines and the rain falls. He originally understood it through music, which gave him the discipline and desire to apply his skills to other undertakings. A true master of one thing can use that understanding to be a master of almost anything. Successful pursuit of purpose in life becomes the ability to follow the flow of our heart's deepest desire for meaning and be brave enough to follow the path unfolding in our spirit, especially when it calls us to take the decision to shift our career to a new area of interest as our purpose evolves.

In a seminal work that describes the conflict between social conditioning and our individual quest for meaning, Anna Miller-Tiedeman wrote of the elusive and sometimes quirky path to purpose in her book "How to Not Make It and Succeed." She described an analogy put forth by a sportswriter of the times: At birth we are given a rickety old folding card table and a deck of cards and our original purpose in life is to set up the table and arrange the cards in a manner to our liking. Most people, even if they do manage to arrange their cards, will then sit back in a comfortable chair to admire their accomplishment for the rest of their lives. Authentic, purpose-driven leaders are different. They are brave enough to take a last, admiring look at their card table and then give it a swift kick so that the table collapses and the cards fly into chaos. At that point they have given themselves the unique opportunity to start over, to set up the table and arrange the cards once again, but in a newly evolved way.

It takes courage to kick one's card table, but the music in Ervin's soul has allowed him to keep kicking away, from pianist, to philosopher-writer, to social activist. The will and vision it took to do this comes so naturally that it seems easy to the reader, although it is anything but that, and as such, there is a gentle hero's story theme to Ervin's journey. Extraordinary as it is, his story seems the most likely story ever told.

Purpose unfolds in both the material world and the realm of consciousness. Coherence and complexity do their long, slow work in physics and biology to produce creatures such as Homo sapiens. Then we journey through multiple incarnations in this life and perhaps others, so that finally love and oneness gain increasing presence in our mind, reaffirming the prior unity from which our universe arose. The ultimate meaning of our life unfolds as a spiritual awakening. It happens when we fully embrace the "holotropic attractor" of purpose and let it guide us to our destination. The original seed of love and oneness that took root in the soil of our soul now blossoms into our ultimate purpose. As a result of such an extraordinary life as Ervin Laszlo has led, we find the final answer. Music, philosophy, and humanitarian-activism have fused into the Cosmic Consciousness of one man's mind, and as a result, purpose itself has evolved to a higher understanding of its own nature.

DAVID LORIMER

"The universal direction taken by evolution is evident throughout the realms of living systems. It is ascension toward higher and higher levels of complexity and coherence in regard to the body, and toward higher and higher levels of oneness and love in regard to the consciousness associated with the body."

—ERVIN LASZLO

It is a privilege and a pleasure to contribute a few reflections on the purpose and meaning of human life to Ervin Laszlo's *My Journey*, just as my own book of 25 essays written over the last 40 years (*A Quest for Wisdom: Inspiring Purpose on the Path of Life*) sees the light of day.

The important part of my story is not the outer events, but the inner spiritual journey and the lessons learned along the way. In Gnosticism and the work of Plotinus, the fall is one into ignorance, forgetfulness and density. I have come to believe that the process/game/play of incarnation involves a degree of forgetting who we are at our core and that the essential quest is one of remembering and awakening.

In the spring of 1985, I bought a book by Omraam Mikhael Aivanhov titled *Cosmic Moral Laws*, which I read on holiday in Crete. It made a deep impression and introduced me to the work of his teacher, the Bulgarian Sage Beinsa Douno (Peter Deunov, 1864–1944). Deunov has been the fundamental shaping influence on my spiritual life. My core daily practices are based on his teachings and on his five fundamental principles of Love, Wisdom, Truth, Justice, and Virtue or Goodness: Love brings Life, Wisdom brings Light, and Truth brings Freedom. He emphasized that the salvation of the world is not to be found in belief systems but in the embodiment and application of these universal principles.

This brings me to the header quotation about evolution from Ervin's essay: the movement towards higher levels of complexity, coherence, oneness and love. This corresponds to my own understanding of the direction of cultural evolution. In a recent book he has a contribution from Barbara Marx Hubbard (1929–2018) who writes that "a universal human is one who is connected through the heart to the whole of life, attuned to the deepest intelligence of nature, and called forth irresistibly by Spirit to express his or her gifts creatively in the evolution of self and the world." She adds: "We are evolving in the recurring evolutionary direction as individuals, towards greater consciousness, freedom and loving order. The inner motivation of most evolving humans is towards expanded consciousness, greater freedom, and deeper access to complex order, connecting in love."

These are the very same principles at work as expressed by Deunov and they call us all to engage in deep alignment and a radical cultural renewal to bring to birth a new culture of Love,

Wisdom, Truth, Justice, and Goodness. He writes: "Life is one, Mind is one, Love is one . . . All beings form a whole as branches and leaves of the great cosmic tree of the cosmic organism—so Love is Life for the Whole." Hence "the supreme goal of human life is that people should be free and to serve Love, Wisdom and Truth. These new people will think of the good of our neighbors as their own good. Now is the time for the strong to manifest Love, to give all the warmth and light of Love."

I strive to embody these principles within my being and also in my relationships with others while following the sense of my soul blueprint as it unfolds. I have a strong sense of historic connection to the mystical tradition of gnosis, for instance as witness by the Cathars of Languedoc, the region in which I live. I am still a heretic by orthodox standards in a number of respects, which for me means taking an independent stand for truth over unexamined received opinions, propaganda and manipulation. In my life and work, what matters to me is developing a compassionate universal viewpoint and being of loving service to the whole. One manifestation of this is my Inspiring Purpose project for schools. This work helps young people live from the inside out and to define their goals and aspirations. The project has reached over 350,000 young people.

Perhaps I can summarize my views and comments in a poem.

Deliverance

Every year the Earth
Gives birth to new life—
But what about us?
Can we give birth
To a new culture,
A culture of love
A culture of wisdom
A culture of truth
A culture of justice
A culture of freedom
A culture of kindness
A culture of peace
A culture of beauty?
Or will we remain
Huddled in darkness
Trapped in fear
Stifled by control
Cowed into compliance
Canceled by censors—
Unable to breathe freely,
Sleepwalking backwards
Into digital slavery?

Deep grief wells up—
A sense of human future lost,
Of time being short,
Earth in the balance,
Breakdown and breakthrough
Coming into view.

Will this culture of hope
Be stillborn again?
Or can we finally deliver
This new world together
With courage and love?

The Earth has long awaited
This moment of deliverance
From violence and secrecy,
From deception and evil.

The world can torture
And crucify the good
But the light of love
Endures,
Comes through—
Human hearts crack open,
The birth pangs of one humanity
Awakening oh so slowly,
Agonizingly
Emerging
From the cave of suffering
To greet the rising sun.

Masami Saionji

In *My Journey: A Life in Quest of the Purpose of Life*, Ervin Laszlo offers us a rare and precious treasure—one that can open new doors for us as we each guide ourselves forward on our path in life.

Having achieved great success as a concert pianist, Ervin found himself searching for an additional purpose in life. He writes, "The commonsense way to follow up on my new-year's (or new-life's) resolution would have been to take philosophy courses at a university: the University of Munich in the city where we lived at the time, could have met this requirement. But I postponed enrolling until later. First, I wanted to reach down and understand my experience on my own. I had an intuitive sense that the answer is in me, if only I could uncover it." Having formed this intention, he began devoting time each day to typing out whatever thoughts flowed through his mind. This, I feel, was done in order to draw out and further develop the precious insights that were circulating there.

To me, this state of mind is exactly what we need to have when we seriously wish to search for the purpose of our life. Before listening to what others have to say, or before enrolling in a course of study, I feel that we first need to draw out our own inner wisdom, and trust it. Before seeking the opinions of others, I think we need to tune in to the insights that were born of our own experiences and awareness. If we live in this way, there is no doubt that our inner wisdom will respond to the trust we placed in it. Intuitive guidance will spring forth from within, opening up our path step by step.

As we continue our quest, we may also wish to read books or search the internet for information that resonates with our experience and our heart's desire. We may start developing opportunities to meet people who hold similar aims to ours. However, from the beginning our stance has to be grounded in a deep awareness that the answers we seek are concealed within us, waiting to be uncovered. Otherwise, those answers will never be found. Even if noble truths are conveyed to us by excellent teachers or experts in various fields, we will not be able to put those truths into practice and make them our own.

Another lesson to be learned from Ervin's journey is for us to follow a path that brings joy to our heart. If we are tracing a path that was determined by others—a path we accepted because we believed in others more than we did in ourselves—it will be hard for us to live our lives with happiness and enthusiasm. Even if our chosen path holds more challenges than we wished for, our heart will be sustained by the courage and sense of commitment that we nurtured along the way.

The most distressing issue that I see with people who lead joyless lives is a tendency to underestimate their own self-worth. It is an inexpressibly grave error for us to believe that we lack talent or integrity, or that our own ideas and experiences do not have much meaning.

Whether we are conscious of it or not, each and every one of us is born with a vast reservoir of capabilities and a deep desire to be of service to others. I say this because we each hold the very same essential consciousness within us. At the profoundest level, we are one and the same life—one and the same being. We are like the organs, muscles, nerves, and life's blood that make up one living body. Although our individual roles may be different, we share the same intrinsic identity; we are meant to work in unison for the perfect health of the whole.

Each of us, without exception, has something of immense value to contribute to the world—something that no one else can offer. We must never give up doing this. Even if we have only one day left to live, we must live that one day with the knowledge that we are indispensable to the world. By means of our thoughts, our words, and our life-energy, each of us is working ceaselessly to create a more highly evolved, harmonized world—an infinitely diverse world filled with limitless potential.

What do I mean when I talk about an "essential consciousness?" I am speaking about what exists at the source of everything. Our essential consciousness is the source of harmony, the source of love, the source of intelligence, and the source of creation. And by creation, I mean something like "vibrations." In Japanese spiritual teachings, these creative vibrations are called kotodama (言霊), which means "the spirit of words." In the Bible, they are called "Word." (I refer to the book *Essays on the Bible* by Masahisa Goi.)

The creative vibrations that we human beings are sending out are none other than the words we speak and the thoughts we think each day. Just by thinking thoughts and speaking words, we human beings are creating the conditions and the relationships that are spreading across the planet and through the universe. And so, it seems to me that our purpose in this world is to think thoughts and speak words that express only what is good and harmonious. In so doing, we will be able to develop societies and cultures in which all beings live in mutual respect, harmony, love, and happiness.

In this critical period in Earth's history, the future of the planet is hanging in the balance. Whether or not we can safely enter the next stage of Earth's development will depend on the daily thoughts and words of each and every human being. Let us continue to do our best to the very last moment. May peace prevail on Earth!

MICHAEL SANDLER

Ervin Laszlo's story is about reinvention, reincarnation, and what I call following the flow-line of life and seeing where the doors open or close, and being brave enough to step through. To me, we each receive these universe-calls, but we rarely pick up the receiver. I can see great parallels between Ervin's life and my own. And wow, has he made the most of his life!

My turn has come not with melodic whispers, but with large concussive thuds: I have had several severe accidents, including two near-death experiences, each giving me a profound glimpse into the cosmos and the fabric of life, far beyond my years of understanding. They each completely changed me. They were both iterative, yet giant leaps, and there was no going back.

Most importantly, like Ervin, who uses his ability to write the flow and tap into the Akashic Field, I learned how to tune in, and now teach it through AWE, the Automatic Writing Experience because the wisdom of the field should be accessible to everyone.

Whether it is Ervin's life, my life, or yours, life is not iterative. People think of it as linear, people think of it as do a, go to b, have c . . . but nothing could be further from the truth. Life is not iterative; it is a bunch of points on a map, it is electron state changes, it is raising to higher levels of vibration or energy, from which one can never go back.

When we are talking about the purpose of life, we are talking about a web, a network, whole and complete, where everything is in the middle, and there is no edge. . . . everything is one, always growing, always expanding, always learning, always vibrating at a higher frequency . . .

Life is alive, and everything is life. . . .

Everything is always seeking a higher state of being, a higher state of consciousness, a higher state of complexity, and a higher state of awareness. Everything, from the "lifeless" rock to the human, to the sun, to the galaxies themselves, is alive, everything has awareness, everything has intelligence, everything has consciousness, and everything is energy. . . .

For everything is no-thing, and everything is one.

At the bottom line, there are no galaxies, planets, rocks, or even us . . . we are simply energy, organized on this holographic image that we imagine into beingness as something that is real. . . . Now there is a realness to it, there is a consciousness, there is a coherence, there is a cogent nature that brings it all together . . . And this is love . . .

When we talk about fields, scientists often stay away from the term "love" as it is too soft, but Ervin has not steered away, and nor do I, for we are all bathed in the field of pure love, and even fleeting brief glimpses of it are driving forces in our lives.

Love is everything, love is expansion, and love is the purpose and meaning of life. . . . love is ever expanding nature. . . .

for it is the one energy that the more that it gives, the more of it comes back. . . . there is never an exhaustion of love, there is never a limit to how much one can love, and there is never a limit to how much love there is in the universe. . . . Love is both infinite in supply and ever growing. . . .

Yes, life is full of paradoxes, that is its very nature…life is to be both infinite and ever expanding, like the universe itself. . . .

What does this mean, why is love ever expanding, to know itself, to grow ever stronger, to expand consciousness, the awareness that's all that is. To ask what is on the other side of love is like asking what is on the other side of the big bang.

The meaning and purpose of life is to help expand love, that is what it is all about. On the microscopic level there is love, on the macroscopic level there is love. Love is infinite in all directions. The sun pours her heat out with love. The galaxies do their cosmic dance with love. All there is the song of love, the vibratory harmony of love, in each and every moment.

While I never expected that I would do so, I am continuously talking about angels, and about vibrating at a higher frequency—I am talking about being at a higher octave of love, for one is always in vibrational alignment, one is always in harmony, but there are different states, different energy levels, and these differences are octaves. And so the greater meaning of life, from this metaphorical and metaphysical point of view, is to live and play and sustain the highest octave we can, and then to expand to the next octave and the next and the next, moving upward, to higher and higher octaves. This is the cosmic spiral. It is like playing scales on the piano. . . . go harmoniously around and around, spiraling upwards from one octave, to the next and to the next.

It may look to the observer that life is merely cycling, stuck in time, like the planets, always coming back to the exact starting point. But the universe is ever expanding. It is continuously expanding in one direction: upwards . . .

How can there be an up, when there is no down, and how can there be an in when there is no out? This is the paradox of the universe. Yet the universe is always growing to a more coherent state, always growing to more and more complex music, to a higher and higher octave. It is as simple as this. The universe is alive, she is music, and she herself is the symphony, always seeking to play at the highest level . . .

This is what Ervin Laszlo discovered—and that is the meaning for all of us . . . to live the music, to be the music, to breathe the music, to perfuse the music . . . and to raise consciousness by being the harmony, being one with the music itself.

Are all of us the music? Yes, there is nothing that is not the music, that is missing in this paradigm. Yet we are in a state of amnesia, or of hypnosis, or a deep sleeping state. How could the note c-flat think it is any less important than the c-sharp, how could a major chord think she is better than a minor chord . . .?

Group think keeps us in a perpetual state of confusion, a state of electron frenzy, of "disorder." Of course, as we have seen in this book, there is no such thing as absolute disorder, chaos, it is simply a rearranging of the energy, a re-composition of the music that drives us to a higher state . . . From the inside it looks chaotic, but from the outside it is a charging of the rocket, it is the shaking of a bottle of which once the top is released, it is jetting to a higher state . . . The propulsion is instant, a flash from one octave to the next, but there is an energy building up, for a powerful state change. Could that energy be directed elsewhere, as in the bifurcation of humanity Ervin discusses . . . is that up to the Zeitgeist, the collective spirit of humanity?

Whether humanity goes on her own ride spiraling upwards, or remains simply part of the shake-up of the cosmic bottle, just one fleeting note in the symphony of the universe, humanity matters, for every note matters, every pebble matters, every being matters, now and forever. Every part of existence, from a glass bottle to the atoms you breathe in the air, is part of the concert, part of the performance, part of life itself.

Life. It matters.

KARAN SINGH

Ervin Laszlo's journey starts with being a musical prodigy making his debut with the Budapest Philharmonic at the age of nine and continuing to win international prizes. Music for him was essentially a spiritual experience and he could well have spent the rest of his life as an outstanding pianist. However, his inner self wanted to probe deeper into the mystery of existence, as a result of which he morphed into a profound thinker and philosopher.

His journey has been a fascinating one. It illustrates, among other things, the close connection between music and the higher consciousness, a phenomenon well-known in Hindu philosophy. Indeed, music is believed to be the fastest path to divine realization in those who worship any of the divinities of the Hindu pantheon. In Christianity also, there have been some saints who excelled in music, and this is particularly significant in the Islamic Sufis, whose whirling ecstatic dance is well known.

There are thus numerous examples of saints across the religious realms who achieved their enlightenment through the sheer power of music and dance. The sacred word is called in Sanskrit "mthe shabd brahm," the divine word. The dance of Shiva, the Nataraja, is a marvelous demonstration of the creative fusion of music, rhythm, and percussion.

This slim but fascinating book by Laszlo on his spiritual journey is a joy to read. The deeper question of the purpose of human life on Earth that he explores is at the heart of the Upanishads, these sublime dialogues between realized masters and earnest students represent a high watermark not only of Hindu but of world philosophy. For example, the Kena Upanishad, written around 1000 BC, opens with the following questions "who makes my mind think? who fills my body with vitality? who causes my tongue to speak? who is that invisible one who sees through my eyes and hears through my ears? The Upanishad goes on to affirm:

> The Self is realized in a higher state
> Of consciousness when you have broken through
> The wrong identification that you are
> The body, subject to birth and death
> To be the Self is to go beyond death
> Realize the Self, the shining goal of life!

Writing in *The Wisdom Principles* (and already cited in this book), Laszlo says:

> The key to understanding the purpose of existence is the recognition that we are not biophysical but psychophysical entities. On the one hand, we are bodies: matter-like vibrations in the cosmic field. But on the other, we are mind-like vibrations—intrinsic parts of the consciousness that pervades the universe.

What is particularly interesting in Laszlo's work is the manner in which he has sought to harmonize, if not to integrate, the experience of higher consciousness with the latest scientific developments. Today, the traditional rigid exclusivist form of religion is gradually giving way to the acceptance of the great Rig Vedic dictum: "The Truth is one, the wise call it by many names." Hinduism is perhaps the only religion that has, from its inception, accepted multiple paths to the divine, which surely has to be the basis of the Interfaith Movement. In a parallel development, the rigid dichotomy of Newtonian/Cartesian physics has been superseded by the insights of Einstein and Heisenberg. It now appears that all matter ultimately dissolves into energy, and this bring it closer to the view that spirituality expresses itself not so much in outer ritual, as in the growth of a higher consciousness.

Today the cutting edge of research involves the study of consciousness, the critical question of its evolution. Sri Aurobindo holds that man is an intermediate creature between the animal and the divine; that he does not represent the culmination but just a step in the adventure of evolution. The further evolution from mind to super-mind, is the inevitable thrust of destiny.

There are alternative visions. For example, Arthur Koestler holds that man is in fact a species doomed to self-destruction because of an engineering defect in the human cortex so that the thinking and feeling capacities are not adequately harmonized. As a result, while we know what should be done, we do not in fact do it. This is chillingly evident in our approach to the ongoing disaster of climate change and global warming. The jury is still out regarding these the alternative projections. Perhaps on a lighter note I could recall a limerick I learnt long ago:

> God's plan is to make a hopeful beginning
> But Man spoilt his chances by sinning
> We know that the story
> Will end in God's glory
> But at present the other side is winning

Be that as it may, in his long and productive life Ervin Laszlo has given us a large number of valuable books articulating and elaborating his worldview. When he founded the Club of Budapest, I was among the first to join as one of his friends. Because we live on different continents, I have not been able to play as active a role as I would have liked, but we have, kept in touch with each other over the decades. The Club of Budapest has been envisaged as the culture/philosophy counterpart of the Club of Rome, which concentrated mainly on economic and political issues.

Laszlo has gathered a number of distinguished thinkers from around the world for the purpose of deepening the dialogue between science and spirituality. This is an undertaking that could have a profound influence on the future of the human species. I commend this slender volume to all who seek a deeper purpose in life and are striving to attain a higher consciousness.

MICHAEL CHARLES TOBIAS

When Ervin Laszlo and I sat down for six days at his home in Tuscany to engage in conversation that was to become our book, *The Tuscany Dialogues*,* I did not know at that time about his wonderful moment of transcendent apprehension, as it were, when he sat down many years before to perform Beethoven's Sonata opus 53, the "Waldstein Sonata," only to be caught up in a revelatory cloud of Knowing/Unknowing, as I might interpolate from his extraordinary description of it in this book. I can easily relate to that moment because when I was around nine-years old I gave my last public performance on the piano (although I would continue to study classical music and play the piano for my entire life). It was supposed to be a few Mozart Sonatinas. Needless to say, I had neither the extensive training, talent, discipline nor anywhere near the experience of Ervin at nine to get through this profoundly disorienting sense that I was floating off the stage, into the stars, the forests, the seas. I found myself in a total state of perplexed and indeed fascinating hallucination-like mode of being.

Stage fright? No. I knew these Sonatinas sufficiently well, by rote. It was the fact that I had just recently finished reading Jean-Paul Sartre's *La Nausée* in which the existentialist hero, Antoine

---

* SelectBooks/EcologyPrime, New York, 2019.

Roquentin, encounters the bark of a chestnut tree in a park within the imaginary town of Bouville and is forever shaken to his own roots by the very fact of biology. There I was an absolutely shaken boy literally trembling with a sensation he could not explain. As I recall, the concert did not go well. To make matters worse, my Grandmother Dora, had warned me that reading J. P. Sartre was more dangerous than "doing marijuana."

But I went on to devour the literary, philosophical and scientific realms surrounding the surrealism of Sartre and his visionary quest to nonetheless understand the life we all share.

Fifty-five years later, my wife Jane and I had the great pleasure of getting to know Ervin and Carita through the Club of Budapest. By that time, I had spent more than a half-century searching to understand biological evolution and human consciousness, doing ecological field research on many continents, in more than a hundred states, in numerous and puzzling alpine cirques, along countless watersheds and in thousands of microbiomes. Throughout this odyssey, I, too, like Ervin have sought feverishly to make sense of what is happening. Is there a purpose? Does our meager consciousness and erratic conscience stem from forces beyond our humble grasp? Is there an explanation within the evolutionary scientific corpus that can explain both Mozart's *Marriage of Figaro* and the Holocaust?

There is a reason I put the former in quotation marks, but not the latter. Human nature, and indeed, all of nature, is both brutal and remarkable; fickle and emphatically unfair; exquisite and horrifying. There are mathematical explanations and theories, not to mention a raft of well-known paradoxes that attempt to make sense of uncertainty; to glean coherence out of incoherence; to endeavor to stamp order on chaos and provide both particles and waves as clever explanations for a number of seemingly universal phenomena, including what Ervin calls "the holotropic attractor."

When working on *The Tuscany Dialogues*, Ervin was consistently driven by the idea that "The purpose of evolution in the finite universe is the union of the consciousness that evolves in space and time with the beyond-spacetime infinite intelligence that is the cosmos itself."

"But what about suffering?" I persisted in asking. "The Anthropocene—the sixth biodiversity extinction spasm humanity alone has unleashed upon the world? Does the comos even notice?"

This pivotal bifurcation point, quietly and with astonishing faith Ervin continued to argue, makes sense in a cosmic scheme, and not necessarily just for us. He paraphrased Plato who said that all statements about the real world are but likely stories. "My credo is the scheme, the set of insights, that makes up the likeliest story."

We had a fascinating discussion about this key point, particularly with respect to "purpose." I have always held that the anthropic lens through which humanity continues to view itself (as implausibly "superior" to the rest of all biodiversity) undermines our ability to see straight. We do not have the vantage point of either a bacterium or a Giant Sequoia. Indeed, our collective perspectives have not worked, certainly not in terms of the inordinately violent, reckless mayhem we have meted out to a vast number of our fellow sentient beings.

Not disagreeing, Ervin always pointed to a higher level of reckoning that I continue to find challenging. The notion that the erratic bio-histories of our species are going through something profound; that our instincts are not always wrong; that unconditional love is a vibrational echo of a working cosmic principle we can at least vaguely glimpse however self-correcting, are utterly revolutionary and challenging.

As quantum bio-physics moves closer and closer in its insights to a Mozart, a Darwin, an Aristotle, we can indeed recognize the prospect that Ervin has been reiterating with greater and greater depth throughout his spiritual journey. Our species is indeed flawed, but it is not an empty vessel. As with all other biological quanta, *H. sapiens* is a vivid proof that we may well have what it takes to pour forth our hearts in a communion with the cosmos and the fantastic, illimitable urgings of forces that, from our first inception, we have pre-consciously inculcated. Ervin remains a great champion of them.

FREDERICK TSAO

Our world has been dominated for over two hundred years by the materialistic, deterministic and dualistic ideas of Isaac Newton and Adam Smith. These have well served the industrialization era, and we have enjoyed the fruits of its development. Today, we are in need of a global common belief system, and globalization provides an integration point of the different world views and systems. However, we lack a common language and the one presented by Ervin Laszlo can finally provide an opportunity for a science-based language to bridge the today's differing worldviews. Quantum science bridges physics and metaphysics, and the new science of consciousness is the new science of life. Ervin's wisdom has put forth a new modern-age scientific paradigm that validates the cultural tradition-based practices of the East.

It is not a coincidence that the ancient Chinese cultural tradition is consistent with the modern scientific view of evolution and life. Chinese culture has the concept of cause and effect, karma, consciousness and fate (*mingyun* 命运), expressed in *lúnhuí* 輪回 (the closest English word for *lúnhuí* 輪回 is "metempsychosis"), which is like a fractal geometry, an energy that moves in cycles, as a natural spiral. The Chinese believe in all these concepts, and in the spiral movements *lúnhuí* 輪回. At the core of creation is the Dao 道, an evolutionary and creative energy, originating from the field or ultimate nothingness called wuji 無極. It is the Dao that gives birth to yin-yang 陰陽, the vibrational energy of the creation of all things Taiji 太極. The Chinese tradition also offers a blueprint for life[1] in the *Huangdineijing* 黃帝內經. This describes the entire creation process with its different layers ranging from the universe to the smallest element of life.

The essence (*jing* 精) of heaven is the Dao—it dances with the energy (*qi* 氣) of the Earth, with the entering divinity (*shen* 神) which, when combined, is Jing-Qi-Shen 精氣神, essence. Energy and divinity create human life form, giving birth to the soul (the Chinese word for it is *Po* 魄), the energy body which gives birth to the physical body and the mind. The mind is the creator of all reality, the locus of intention and the unfolding of the inner world in outer expression. The rise of intention creates consciousness which orients the will for the emergence of thought. In the Chinese cultural tradition, at the tip of the ice-berg consciousness takes off from ideas and knowing. This, when combined with the five roots (五根) of sensory receptors (sight, hearing, taste, touch and smell) forms the six roots (六根) of our conscious world. In the reverse spiral these are the same roots to connect with the consciousness path toward oneness, leading back to the Dao. Consciousness at this level rises from our journey into the inner world, where in being mindful in stillness we become conscious of the sub-conscious, and the unconscious realm vibrates toward a state of oneness and love.

From the consciousness of the mind and through the mind back to the soul, and back all the way to Dao and eventually to *wuji* 無極, the ultimate nothingness.

The Dao is constantly creating in these two spirals; it produces a pattern. The pattern of the Dao is the yin-yang movement that creates all material things. We can think of the yin-yang movement as vibrational energy. When we look at vibrational energy in 3-dimensions, it is like a spiral—whereas in 2-dimension, it is like a sine curve. The 3-dimensional spiral appears everywhere in our material world—it is expressed in nature and in our DNA. The rhythm of this vibrational energy crosses the material and the spiritual realms, dancing in harmony and creating, interplaying with essence and form: *lúnhuí* 輪回. Whatever name we may give it, whether it is Dao, or as Ervin proposes the holotropic attractor, it is the same: it is the deeper "something" in the world.

Everything must be in sync with the rhythm and spiral in *lúnhuí* 輪回. This is expressed in the most important Chinese classic as, the *I-Ching*,[2] *Daodejing*,[3] and *Huangdineijing*.[4,5] The traditional-cultural and the modern-scientific paradigms are congruent in the interpretation of the evolution of consciousness. One journey inside is guided by traditions and another journey outside is led by science. So, I can say that the Chinese perspective of evolution as the real nature of existence is consistent with Ervin's scientific perspective on evolution. Both views are consistent in that evolution is the purpose of life, and evolution conduces to higher level of complexity and coherence, toward the integration its holistic essence while constantly developing and aligning impelled by oneness and love. Self-cultivation is the Chinese traditional cultural practice of shifting consciousness through living in harmony with the impetus of the universe, and uniting with the source of creation, the Dao. The physical world and the Dao are inseparable as the mind creates the physical world.

Ervin's wisdom provides the key to re-opening the gate that humanity has shut with its ignorant choices of life, neither natural nor aligned with the purpose of our existence. This opens the way for humanity to cultivate a state of well-being, described by traditional Chinese wisdom as one where every system creates naturally and is flourishing. Humans need to awaken to the realization that the current way of living has created separate and unsustainable languages, beliefs, worldviews and cultures. These must be integrated as we cannot be well unless the whole system is well, unless we are in oneness with the universe *tianrenheyi* 天人合. Whether it is East or West, ancient or modern, these are but different words that have the same meaning. These are exciting times for humanity and the world, as the perspective presented by Ervin is an opportunity for the development of a common science-based language to bridge today's differing worldviews, and create a unifying force for humanity to reach a new way of life in an era of wellbeing. Reaching that way of life and thus an era of well-being could be the ultimate purpose of human life.

NEALE DONALD WALSCH

While estimates range widely, most demographers agree that about 100 billion human beings have lived on Earth over the course of human history. Because a significant number never reached adulthood, I'll use a lower figure for my next statement. I'm going to guesstimate that no less than 80 billion people have asked themselves the question that has occupied Ervin Laszlo's mind for the largest part of his life.

Who among us has not stared at the ceiling, or out some window, or at our reflection in the mirror, and pondered at least once: "What in the world am I doing here? What is the point of this? What is my purpose?"

So while the astonishing thinking of Mr. Laszlo through the years indisputably scores high on the originality scale, the question he has asked here most decidedly does not. Ah, but a genius is someone who dares to provide answers here and now to questions everyone else has been asking forever.

Ervin Laszlo has spent most of his life being called a genius. And understandably so, for his remarkable ruminations have been consistently breathtakingly insightful.

Now, on this particular topic, what do I think about what he thinks?

Who cares, one might exclaim—and there could scarcely be a more legitimate protest. It's a bit like asking the bat boy if he thinks Babe Ruth was swinging correctly. Or inquiring of the stagehand how he feels about Laurence Olivier's Hamlet. I have, nonetheless, been invited by Ervin himself to offer a reflection on his reflections here, and so, I've humbly placed my speculations alongside his.

For me, the question of purpose is tied intrinsically to that of identity. It's a question I've grown to feel must be answered by everyone who wishes to make some sense of their life. So I'm going to ask you here: Who are you?

Or as my father put it to me repeatedly from my 9th birthday until my 17th: "Who do you think you are, anyway?"

I don't know if Dad held it as the most significant question of all time, but I've come to believe it is. And there was a point in my life when I felt the need to ask myself: Who am I?

Really.

Who am I?

Am I a physical entity, not unlike a bird in the sky or a fish in the sea? More sophisticated, perhaps. More complex, possibly. But a chemical creature, essentially? A corporeal life form?

Or is it possible that I am something more than that? Could it be that I am a spiritual entity? Might the reality be that my True Self, my Total Identity, is metaphysical, not merely physical?

If that is the reality, it opens up more questions about my life. Not only asking what my purpose is here, but what is the meaning of that purpose in the overall scheme of things? What does what I'm doing have to do with who I am?

For me, the surprising answer is: Nothing.

This has led me to another inquiry, one that I've been posing in my own books and everywhere I've gone for the past 25 years: Is it possible that there is something we don't fully understand about life, about God, and about ourselves, the understanding of which would change everything?

My answer is yes, and what I have come to realize is that life is not about what I am doing; it's about what I am being. It is not about what I am up to; it's about what I am up for.

I have concluded that I am a spiritual being. I am not my body. My body is something I have. I am not my mind; my mind is something I use. I am what some religions would call a soul—an individuation of the Essential Essence that I have come to call Divine.

Yes, I believe there is a First Cause. I believe there's an Ultimate Source of an Organizing Principle that expresses in countless variations, but with absolute consistency, throughout the cosmos. In short, I believe in God.

I am comfortable with that word because I have come to experience God as self-aware, self-conscious energy, the expression of which is a process that we call Life. I do not see the Higher Power as a great big Being in the sky who is going to judge, condemn, and punish us if we don't obey commands, but as an intricate system of singular energetic vibrational emanations producing the characteristics of all physical objects, and generating energy exchanges between those objects in a cause-and-effect relationship that creates events in the physical realm.

It is my hypothesis that all physical objects and life forms react to these vibrations, with sentient beings able to respond in a way which expresses their understanding, knowing, and choice about who they are and how they elect to experience any given moment—an ability befitting spiritual entities individuating Divinity.

I hold the idea that there is no separation between The Source and That Which Is Sourced. And the purpose of life? To me it feels like something as simple, and as complex, as evolution. And I observe that humans, as sentient beings, express the greatest and most meaningful aspects of Life through what they are being, not through what they are doing.

It feels to me that it is through the expression of our Essential Essence (which I call Pure Love)—whether we are giving seeds to the birds in our backyard or planting seeds in peoples' minds in audiences of hundreds—that we experience aspects of our Total Identity. It feels, as well, that it is through the never-ending expansion in the sharing of this Essential Essence that we evolve.

I observe here that this process of our species' evolution advances every time Ervin Laszlo opens a topic of conversation with his formidable forays into life's deepest mysteries.

Most people don't talk enough about these kinds of things. But the esteemed Mr. Laszlo has spent decades encouraging humanity to do so, inviting us to join him in tackling life's most meaningful questions, dissecting our interconnected philosophical and theological understandings, and engaging mutually and collegially in exploratory excursions.

If this is not one of the most powerful ways that evolution advances, then I don't know what is.

GARY ZUKAV

When I read Ervin Laszlo saying that consciousness defines the cosmos, that it is all consciousness, that consciousness is all there is and cosmic consciousness is beyond limitation in space and time, and that it is a sea of potentialities—an undifferentiated wholeness—I was thrilled, for my experience had brought me to the same conclusion as Ervin's, whom I greatly admire.

I am not educated in physics, apart from a book I authored forty-three years ago, so I cannot comment on Ervin's amazing description of his perceptions, or perhaps conclusions. I do not know what a ground state is, but I know the Universe is consciousness, and there is nothing else. The Universe is all that is and all that is not, all that can be comprehended and all that cannot be comprehended. It is us; it is the Earth, and it is every form of matter, thought, and all else. I say these things with faith, for they express my experiences, yet I do not say that my experiences are other than my experiences—precious, as are yours, and as are all others.

In my experience, no single perception can encompass the Universe, and the points of possible perception are without number—hence my experiences and yours and Ervin's and boundless others. Ervin's perceptions especially resonate with me because his words so accurately express my experiences. I do not say that consensus defines a reality, much less the Universe, for if anything defines a reality, it is the heart, regardless of how forcefully the intellect declares otherwise. In my experience, intentions create experiences, and the reality that we call physical is defined by duality, as well as space, time, and matter. The fundamental duality in it is love and fear. All intentions are one or the other, and all experiences are created by one or the other.

This gives me great joy, because, if it is so for others as it is so for me, we can consciously choose the experiences that we will create by consciously choosing the intention behind each of our words and deeds. Love (for example, gratitude, appreciation, caring, contentment, patience, and awe of the Universe) creates blissful and constructive consequences. Fear (for example, jealousy, anger, vengefulness, righteousness, superiority, and inferiority) creates painful and destructive consequences. These are my experiences, but if they were hypothetical assertions, their unvarying correlation with experience would need to be verified in the laboratories (lives) of any other scientist in the world, anywhere, at any time to be accepted as a theory. The intention of love must always create constructive blissful experiences, and the intention of fear must always create destructive and painful experiences. Sharing our experimental results in this way with one another would co-create the literature of a new and different physics.

We can interpret the possible dynamics that underlie our experimental results—and so far mine have been consistent—in different ways, just as the quantum theory can be, and is, interpreted in different ways (e.g., the Copenhagen Interpretation, the Many Worlds Interpretation). None of them are demonstrably THE interpretation of this theory. As Einstein declared in his famous metaphor of a man attempting to understand the mechanism of a closed watch, we can observe the face and the hands of a watch moving, and might be ingenious enough to form a picture of the mechanism that explains our observations. But we can never open the watch to see if our image is the only one that can explain what we observed.

I am attracted to quantum mechanics because it is an intellectual construction that challenges the hegemony of the intellect (e.g., Bohr's theory of Complementarity and Heisenberg's Uncertainty Principle.) Einstein dismissed it. "[God] does not play dice," he wrote to Max Born in 1926.

I also prefer the Copenhagen Interpretation of the quantum theory, which asserts that it is impossible to know Nature as it "really is." We can only know Nature through our experiments (experiences) with it. This profound conclusion captivated me decades before I was given the gift of experiencing, as I have mentioned, that no one perception of the Universe can encapsulate the Universe.

Shortly after the book that I mentioned above was published, I was invited to a conference on science at a very old university in the Netherlands, not because I was a physicist, but because the theme of the conference was "Against the Grain." In retrospect, I think the organizers may not have realized how much against the grain my book and I were. As I sat on a stage with distinguished colleagues, I mentioned my views about the soul. This was long before I wrote an entire book about them. The audience began to buzz. A young man (we were all young) rose to disdainfully proclaim, "I do not see why Zukav needs a "soul" for his theory." I replied, honestly as I could, "I do not need a soul. I AM a soul, and so are you." The noises of disapproval suddenly became very loud. I felt that I might be experiencing the equivalent of an intellectual lynch mob. Suddenly in the midst of this, a fellow panelist, Douglas Hofstadter, son of a famous scientist, rose to speak. He said about my words something like this: I love music. I like Brahms. I do not like Beethoven, but I recognize great music when I hear it. The magnanimity of his sharing calmed the gathering.

In a similar way, I look upon my experiences and the experiences of others as poetry. I resonate with some more than others, but I recognize great poetry when I hear it. When I read Ervin Laszlo's words, I recognize great poetry. The product of a concert pianist, then a renowned system theorist, and now a proponent for the "Divine Spark" in each of us, the creativity of his poetry (my word, again), in my opinion, calls to all who apply commitment and courage to the expression of their heart's deepest message in language as unique and powerful as their lives.

Thank you, Ervin.

Notes and Bibliography

Notes

1 Paul U. Unschuld, Huang Di Nei Jing, Ling Shu, University of California Press (2016), Chapter 8, "To Consider the Spirit as the Foundation," 146.

2 Wilhelm, R., Baynes, C. F., Jung, C. G., & Francis Bacon Library, (1969). *The I Ching: or, Book of Changes.* Princeton, NJ: Princeton University Press.

3 Chang, Q. Chin. Cult 4, 93–102 (2017) *Translation of Daodejing in English: its place and time.* Int. Commun. https://doi.org/10.1007/s40636 -017-0083-4.

4 Paul U. Unschuld, Huang Di Nei Jing, Ling Shu, University of California Press (2016).

5 Fu W. *The Yellow Emperor's Canon of Medicine: First Complete Summary of Ancient Chinese Medicine.* Chin Med Cult 2018;1:18–20.

Bibliography

Barrow, John D. and Frank J. Tipler. *The Anthropic Cosmological Principle.* Oxford: Clarendon Press, 1986.

Bohm, David. *Wholeness and the Implicate Order.* London: Routledge & Kegan Paul, 1980.

Capra, Fritjof. *The Tao of Physics.* Berkeley: Shambhala Publications, 1975.

Gleick, James. *Chaos: Making a New Science*. New York: Penguin Books, 1988.

Grof, Stanislav. *When the Impossible Happens: Adventures in Non-Ordinary Realities*. Louisville, CO: Sounds True, 2006.

Grof, Stanislav. *A Brief of History of Transpersonal Psychology*, 2008.

Laszlo, Ervin. *The Creative Cosmos: A Unified Science of Matter, Life and Mind*. Edinburg: Floris Books, 1993.

Laszlo, Ervin. *The Interconnected Universe: Conceptual Foundations of Transdisciplinary Unified Theory*. Singapore: World Scientific Publishing Company, 1995.

Laszlo, Ervin. *The Connectivity Hypothesis: Foundations of an Integral Science of Quantum, Cosmos, Life, and Consciousness*. Albany, NY: State University of New York Press, 2003.

Laszlo, Ervin. *Science and the Akashic Field: An Integral Theory of Everything*. Rochester, VT: Inner Traditions, 2007.

Laszlo, Ervin. *What Is Reality: The New Map of Cosmos and Consciousness*. New York: New Paradigm SelectBooks Publisher, 2016.

Pribram, Karl H. *Languages of the Brain*. Englewood Cliffs, NJ: Prentice Hall, 1971.

Prigogine, Ilya. *From Being to Becoming: Time and Complexity in the Physical Sciences*. San Francisco: W. H. Freeman, 1980.

Prigogine, Ilya. and Isabelle Stengers, *Order out of Chaos: Man's Dialogue with Nature*. New York: Bantam Books, 1984.

Sheldrake, Rupert. *A New Science of Life: The Hypothesis of Formative Causation*. Los Angeles, CA: J. P. Tarcher, 1981.

Whitehead, Alfred N. *Process and Reality*. New York: Macmillan, 1967.

Wilber, Ken. *A Theory of Everything: An Integral Vision for Business, Politics, Science and Spirituality*. Berkeley: Shambhala Publications, 2000.

About the Author

photo © by Bernard F. Stehle

ERVIN LASZLO

Ervin Laszlo was born and raised in Budapest. He was a celebrated child prodigy whose public appearances as a pianist began at the age of nine. When he received a Grand Prize at the international music competition in Geneva, he was allowed to cross the Iron Curtain and begin an international concert career, first in Europe and then in America. At the initiative of Senator Claude Pepper of Florida, he was awarded United States citizenship before his 21st birthday by an Act of Congress.

Laszlo received the Sorbonne's highest degree, the *Docteur ès-Lettres et Sciences Humaines* in 1970. Shifting to the life of a scientist and humanist, he lectured and taught at universities in the United States, including Yale, Princeton, Northwestern, the University of Houston, and the State University of New York. Following his work on modeling the future evolution of world order at Princeton, he was asked to produce a report for the Club of Rome, of which he was a member. In the late 70s and early 80s, Laszlo ran global projects at the United Nations Institute for Training and Research at the request of the Secretary-General. In the 1990s his research led him to the discovery of the Akashic Field, which he has continued to study and expound on ever since.

The author, coauthor, or editor of more than 100 books that have appeared in 24 languages, Ervin Laszlo has also published several hundred papers and articles in scientific journals and popular magazines. His autobiography was published in June 2011 under the title *"Simply Genius! And Other Tales from my Life."* Gaia TV produced a special series on his life in the Heritage cycle, and he was the subject of a one-hour PBS television special titled *Ervin Laszlo: Life of a Modern-Day Genius.* He is a member of numerous scientific bodies, including the International Academy of Science, the World Academy of Art and Science, the International Academy of Philosophy of Science, and the International Medici Academy. He was elected member of the Hungarian Academy of Science in 2010. He is Founder and President of The Club of Budapest, an international organization established in 1993 that stands for planetary consciousness and a mission to be a catalyst for the transformation to a sustainable world, and he is the Founder and Director of The Laszlo Institute of New Paradigm Research.

Laszlo is a recipient of various honors and awards, including Honorary PhDs from the United States, Canada, Finland, and Hungary; an Honorary Professorship at the Institute of Technology of Buenos Aires; and Honorary Citizenship of the City of Buenos Aires. He was awarded the Goi Peace Prize of Japan in 2001, the Assisi Mandir of Peace Prize in 2006, the Polyhistor Prize of Hungary in 2015, and the Luxembourg Peace Prize in 2017. He was nominated for the Nobel Peace Prize in 2004 and again in 2005.

Biographical Notes on
the Contributors

GREGG BRADEN

Gregg Braden is a five-time *New York Times* best-selling author, scientist, and pioneer of bridging modern science, social policy, and human potential. His research has led to 15 film credits and 12 award-winning books published in over 41 languages.

Gregg is a member of visionary organizations and think tanks including the American Association for the Advancement of Science (AAAS), the Evolutionary Leadership Organization, The Global Coherence Initiative, and an honorary member of the Club of Budapest. He has presented his discoveries in over 30 countries on six continents and has been invited to speak to The United Nations, Fortune 500 companies, and the U. S. military.

In 2019 he received the Walden Award for New Thought, the Illuminate Award for Conscious Visionaries, and is currently listed on the Watkins Journal as among the top 100 of "the world's most spiritually influential living people" for the 7th consecutive year. His latest books are *The Wisdom Codes* (2020) and *Human by Design* (2019).

ALLAN LESLIE COMBS

Allan Combs, Ph.D., is consciousness researcher, neuropsychologist, and systems theorist at the California Institute of Integral Studies where he is Director of the Consciousness Studies Center. Professor Combs is author and coauthor of over 200 articles, chapters, and books on consciousness and the brain, including *Consciousness Explained Better* endorsed by Ken Wilber as "the finest book on consciousness in modern times." He authored *The Radiance of Being*, with a foreword by Ken Wilber, winner of the best-book award of the Scientific and Medical Network, as well as *Thomas Berry, Dreamer of the Earth*, with Ervin Laszlo. He is Editor of *CONSCIOUSNESS: Ideas and Research for the Twenty-First Century*, and Co-Editor of *The Journal of Conscious Evolution*.

Jude Currivan

Jude Currivan is a cosmologist, planetary healer, futurist, and author, most recently, of *The Cosmic Hologram* published in 2017 and was cofounder of WholeWorld-View also in that year. She was previously one of the most senior business women in the UK. She has a master's degree in physics from Oxford University specializing in quantum physics and cosmology and earned her PhD in archaeology from the University of Reading, specializing in ancient cosmologies. She is a member of the Evolutionary Leaders circle.

Amit Goswami

Amit Goswami, a theoretical quantum physicist, is a retired professor of the University of Oregon's Department of Physics. He is a pioneer of the new paradigm called "science within consciousness," an idea presented in *The Self-Aware Universe*. He has written several popular books based on his research on quantum physics and consciousness, including *Physics of the Soul, The Quantum Doctor, Quantum Creativity*, and *The Everything Answer Book*.

Stanislav Grof

Stanislav Grof, M.D., is a clinical and research psychiatrist. He was Principal Investigator in the psychedelic research program at the Psychiatric Research Institute in Prague and Chief of Psychiatric Research at the Maryland Psychiatric Research Center. Currently he is Professor of Psychology at the California Institute of Integral Studies (CIIS). One of the founders of transpersonal psychology and the founding president of the International Transpersonal Association (ITA), in 2007 he was granted the Vision 97 Award from the Václav and Dagmar Havel Foundation, and in 2010 the Thomas R. Verny Award of the Association for Pre- and Perinatal Psychology. He holds honorary PhD degrees from the Institute of Transpersonal Psychology (ITP), for Psychedelic Therapy and Healing Arts from the Institute of Integral Studies (CIIS) and from the World Buddhist University in Bangkok. He has published over 20 books and 150 journal articles.

Jean Houston

Jean Houston is a futurist and researcher in human capacities, social change, and systemic transformation. She is one of the founders of the Human Potential Movement and has been a key player in the empowerment of women around the world. She is Chancellor of Meridian University and has served on the faculties of Columbia University, Hunter College, Marymount College, The New School for Social Research, and the University of California. She is presently Chair of the United Palace of Spiritual Arts in New York City.

Riccardo Illy

Riccardo Illy is an entrepreneur, former MP of the Italian Parliament, President of the Region Friuli-Venezia Giulia and Major of the City of Trieste. He is a United Kingdom Royal Warrant Holder and Hon. Consul of the French Republic in Trieste.

He is committed to teaching and fostering "disruptive quality." His most recent book is *Così perdiamo il Nord* (*So We Lose the North* [of Italy]), Mondadori, 2008.

Emanuel Kuntzelman

Emanuel Kuntzelman is a social entrepreneur, writer, and inspirational speaker. He founded the Chicago-based nonprofit Greenheart International in 1985 and the Fundación por el Futuro in Madrid, Spain, in

1995. He is also the co-creator of the Global Purpose Movement, which partnered with Unity Earth in 2020 to launch Purpose Earth, an initiative funding projects around the world. Emanuel currently serves on the boards of Integral Transformative Practice International and Unity Earth and is a Senior Advisor to Greenheart, the Laszlo Institute, and A New Republic of the Heart. He is a member of the Evolutionary Leaders Circle, and is co-editor of Purpose Rising (2017).

DAVID LORIMER

David Lorimer is a writer, lecturer, poet, and editor who is a Founder of Character Education Scotland, Programme Director of the Scientific and Medical Network, and former President of Wrekin Trust and the Swedenborg Society. He is the author and editor of over a dozen books, including *Survival? Death as Transition* (1984, 2017) *Resonant Mind* (1990/2017), *The Spirit of Science* (1998), *Thinking Beyond the Brain* (2001), *The Protein Crunch* (with Jason Drew), and *A New Renaissance* (edited with Oliver Robinson). He is Chair of the Galileo Commission. He was awarded a Lifetime Achievement Award as a Visionary Leader by the Visioneers International Network and received the Aboca Human Ecology Prize.

MASAMI SAIONJI

Masami Saionji is Chair of the international peace organizations May Peace Prevail on Earth International, The Goi Peace Foundation, and Byakko Shinko Kai. She continues the work of her adoptive father, Masahisa Goi, who initiated a movement for world peace through the universal prayer May Peace Prevail on Earth. Among the many initiatives she has founded or cofounded are the international Peace Pole Initiative (1986), Symphony of Peace Prayers (2005), the Fuji Declaration (2015), and Soul of WoMen (2016). Mrs. Saionji was named an honorary member of the Club of Budapest (2001) and is the recipient of the Philosopher Saint Shree Dnyaneshwara World Peace Prize (2008), the WON Award honoring distinguished women leaders (2010), the Dr. Barbara Fields Humanitarian Peace Award (2016), and the Luxembourg

Peace Prize (2019). She is the author of numerous books, including *The Principle of Effect and Cause* (2019) and *Essentials of Divine Breathing* (2017).

MICHAEL SANDLER

Michael Sandler is the host of the worldwide Inspire Nation Show, one of the top self-help and spirituality podcasts and YouTube shows, and the YouTube InspireNation Show. He regularly teaches through the Inspire Nation University. His books and his online program are designed help people connect with the field. His latest book is *Awe, The Automatic Writing* Experience (2021).

KARAN SINGH

Dr. Karan Singh is an Indian politician, philanthropist, and poet. He belongs to the Jamwal Dogra Dynasty, the son of the late Maharaja Hari Singh and was the Prince regent of Jammu and Kashmir until 1952. In 1967 he served as cabinet minister in the government of Indira Gandhi. He is a senior member of the Indian National Congress Party serving successively as President and Governor of the former state of Jammu and Kashmir. He was elected Chancellor of Banaras Hindu University for three terms and served till 2018. His latest publication is the book *An Examined Life* (2019).

MICHAEL CHARLES TOBIAS

Michael Charles Tobias is a global ecologist and longtime President of the Dancing Star Foundation committed to the conservation of international biodiversity, animal rights, and environmental education. His most recent books include *On the Nature of Ecological Paradox*, with Jane Gray Morrison (2021).

FREDERICK TSAO

Frederick Tsao is fourth-generation family business leader of IMC Pan Asia Alliance Group. He became chairman in 1995.

With more than 40 years' experience as an entrepreneur, Fred has been conducting research on sustainability and modernity since 1995. His interests embrace Chinese traditional cultural practice and Western quantum science. He founded AITIA Institute and OCTAVE Institute, an integrated well-being business model. His latest publication is *Dawn of an Era of Well-Being*, coauthored with Ervin Laszlo (2021).

NEALE DONALD WALSCH

Neale Donald Walsch is the author of books on contemporary spirituality and modern-day psychology, including seven *New York Times* bestsellers. Before writing *Conversations with God*, he worked variously as a radio station program director, newspaper managing editor, and in marketing and public relations. *Conversations with God*, published in 1995, remained on the *New York Times* Best Seller list for 135 weeks. He has published 28 books translated into 37 languages.

GARY ZUKAV

Gary Zukav is the author of four consecutive *New York Times* bestsellers. He graduated from Harvard and received the Albert Einstein College of Medicine Einstein Award for his Contributions to the Psychosocial Growth of Humanity, the Unity Church Light of God Award, and the World Business Academy Pathfinder Award for his Contribution to the Ongoing Evolution of Knowledge and Consciousness within the Global Business Community. In 1979 he wrote *The Dancing Wu Li Masters: An Overview of the New Physics* and published *The Seat of the Soul* in 1989. His latest book is *Universal Human* (2021).

The Books of Ervin Laszlo, 1963–2021

1963

1. *Essential Society*
   An Ontological Reconstruction
   The Hague: Martinus Nijhoff

2. *Individualism, Collectivism, and Political Power*
   A Relational Analysis of Ideological Conflict
   The Hague: Martinus Nijhoff
   2a. Japanese edition:
   Tokyo: Ochanomizu Shobo, 1985

1966

3. *Beyond Skepticism and Realism*
   An Exploration of Husserlian and Whiteheadian Methods of Inquiry
   The Hague: Martinus Nijhoff

4. *The Communist Ideology in Hungary*
   Handbook for Basic Research
   Dordrecht: D. Reidel
   New York: Humanities Press

5. *Philosophy in the Soviet Union*
   A Survey of the Mid-Sixties (edited)
   Dordrecht: D. Reidel;
   New York: Humanities Press

1969

6. *System Structure and Experience*
   Toward a Scientific Theory of Mind
   New York and London: Gordon & Breach
     6a. Chinese edition:
         Shanghai: Shanghai Translation Publishing House, 1987

1970

7. *La Metaphysique de Whitehead*
   Recherche sur les prolongements anthropologiques
   La Haye: Martinus Nijhoff

8. *Human Values and Natural Science*
   with J. Wilbur (edited)
   New York and London: Gordon & Breach

9. *Human Dignity: This Century and the Next*
   with R. Gotesky (edited)
   New York and London: Gordon & Breach

1971

10. *Human Values and the Mind of Man*
    with J. Wilbur (edited)
    New York and London: Gordon & Breach

11. *Evolution and Revolution*
    Patterns of Development in Nature, Society, Culture and Man
    with R. Gotesky (edited)
    New York and London: Gordon & Breach

1972

12. *Introduction to Systems Philosophy*
    Toward a New Paradigm of Contemporary Thought
    New York and London: Gordon & Breach
    Toronto: Fitzhenry & Whiteside
    Reprinted: Gordon & Breach, 1984
    12a. Pocketbook edition:
         New York, Evanston, San Francisco,
         London: Harper Torchbooks, 1973
    12b. Chinese edition:
         Beijing: The Commercial Publishing House, 1998

13. *The Systems View of the World*
    The Natural Philosophy of the New Developments in the Sciences
    New York: George Braziller, 1972
    Toronto: Doubleday Canada, 1972
    Oxford: Basil Blackwell, 1975
    13a. Persian edition:
         Teheran: Industrial Management Institute, 1975
    13b. Japanese edition:
         Tokyo: Kinokuniya Shoten, 1980
    13c French edition:
         Paris: Librairie des Sciences Techniques Françaises et Etrangères,
    13d. Chinese edition:
         Beijing: Chinese Social Science Press, 1985
    13e. Korean edition:
         Seoul: Chunnam National University Press and
         Bak Youngsa Press, 1986
    13f. Italian edition:
         Genova: Gruppo Editoriale Insieme, 1991

14. *The Relevance of General Systems Theory*
    (edited)
    New York: George Braziller

15. *Emergent Man*
    with J. Stulman (edited)
    New York and London: Gordon & Breach

1974

16. *A Strategy for the Future*
    The Systems Approach to World Order
    New York: George Braziller, 1974
        16a. Japanese edition:
              Tokyo: Sangyo Noritsu Daigaku, 1980
        16b. Korean edition:
              Seoul, 1988

17. *The World System*
    Models, Norms, Applications
    (edited)
    New York: George Braziller

18. *Value Theory in Philosophy and Social Science*
    with J. Wilbur (edited)
    New York and London: Gordon & Breach

1976

19. *Vistas in Physical Reality*
    Festschrift for Henry Margenau
    with E.B. Sellon (edited)
    New York: Plenum Press

1977

20. *Goals for Mankind*
    Report to the Club of Rome on the New Horizons of
        Global Community
    New York: E.P. Dutton, 1977
    Toronto & Vancouver: Clarke, Irwin, 1977
    London: Hutchinson, 1977
        20a. pocketbook edition:
              New York: New American Library
              Signet Books, 1978

20b. Italian edition:
    Milan: Mondadori, 1978
20c. Spanish edition:
    Mexico City: El Manuel Moderno, 1979
20d. Finnish edition:
    Helsinki: Weilin & Goos, 1980
20e. Japanese edition:
    Tokyo: Diamond Publishing, 1980
20f. Serbo-Croation edition:
    Belgrade: Novi Svijet, 1980

21. **Goals in a Global Community**
    Vol. I. Studies on the Conceptual Foundation
    with J. Bierman (edited)
    Oxford and New York: Pergamon Press
    Vol. II. The International Values and Goals Studies
    with J. Bierman (edited)
    Oxford and New York: Pergamon Press
    Czech edition:
    Olomuc: Palacky University

1978

22. **The Inner Limits of Mankind**
    Heretical Reflections on Contemporary Values, Culture and Politics
    Oxford and New York: Pergamon Press, 1978
    paperback edition: London: Oneworld Publications, 1989
    22a. German edition:
        Rosenheim: Horizonte Verlag, 1988
    22b. French edition:
        Paris: Tacor International, 1988
    22c. Italian edition:
        Milano: Feltrinelli, 1990
    22d. Chinese edition:
        Beijing: Social Sciences Academic Press, 2004
    22e. Korean edition:
        Seoul: Kyung Hee University Press, 1979

23. *The Objectives of the New International Economic Order*
   with R. Baker, E. Eisenberg, V.K. Raman
   New York: UNITAR and Pergamon Press
   Reprinted: 1979
   23a. Spanish edition:
       Mexico City: CEESTEM, 1980

24. *The Obstacles to the New International Economic Order*
   with J. Lozoya, J. Estevez, A. Bhattacharya, V.K. Raman
   New York: UNITAR and Pergamon Press
   24a. Spanish edition:
       Mexico City: CEESTEM, 1980

1979

25. *The United States, Canada, and the New International Economic Order*
   with J. Kurtzman (edited)
   New York: UNITAR and Pergamon Press

26. *Western Europe and the New International Economic Order*
   with J. Kurtzman (edited)
   New York: UNITAR and Pergamon Press

27. *The Soviet Union, Eastern Europe, and the New International Economic Order*
   with J. Kurtzman (edited)
   New York: UNITAR and Pergamon Press

28. *Food and Agriculture in the Global Perspective*
   with T. Miljan and J. Kurtzman (edited)
   New York: UNITAR and Pergamon Press

1980

29. **The Structure of the World Economy and Prospects for a New International Economic Order**
    with J. Kurtzman (edited)
    New York: UNITAR and Pergamon Press
    29a. Spanish edition:
        Mexico City: CEESTEM, 1981

1981

30. **Regional Cooperation Among Developing Countries**
    The New Imperatives of Development in the 1980s
    with J. Kurtzman and A. Bhattacharya
    Oxford and New York: Pergamon Press

31. **Political and Institutional Issues of the New International Economic Order**
    with J. Kurtzman (edited)
    New York: UNITAR and Pergamon Press

32. **Disarmament: The Human Factor**
    with D.F. Keys (edited)
    Oxford and New York: Pergamon Press

1983

33. **Systems Science and World Order**
    Selected Studies
    Oxford and New York: Pergamon Press

34. **La Crise Finale**
    Paris: Editions Grasset
    34a. Swedish edition:
        Svenska Dagbladets Förlag, 1984
    34b. Spanish edition:
        Madrid: Debate/Circulo, 1985

154 · MY JOURNEY

34c. Portuguese edition:
Rio de Janeiro: Alves Editora, 1988

1984

35. *Cooperation in the 1980s: Principles and Prospects*
(edited)
London: Cassell-Tycooly

36. *African and Arab Cooperation for Development*
(edited)
London: Cassell-Tycooly

1985

37. *Peace Through Global Transformation*
Hope for a New World in the Late 20th Century
with J.Y. Yoo
Seoul: Kyung Hee University Press

38. *European Culture and World Development*
Unesco Joint Studies for the European Cultural Forum
with I. Vitányi (edited)
Oxford and New York: Pergamon Press;
Budapest: Corvina

1986

39. *Zene—Rendszerelélet—Világrend*
Válogatott Tanulmányok
Budapest: Gondolat

40. *Europe in the Contemporary World*
State-of-the-Art Reports of the United Nations University (edited)
New York and London: Gordon & Breach

1987

41. **Evolution: The Grand Synthesis**
    Boston and London: New Science Library, Shambhala
    41a. Italian edition:
         Milano: Feltrinelli, 1986
    41b. German edition:
         Vienna: Europa Verlag, 1987
    41c. Chinese edition:
         Beijing: Academy of Social Sciences, 1988
    41d. Spanish edition:
         Barcelona: Espasa Calpe, 1988
    41e. French edition: *La Coherence du Réel*
         Paris: Gauthier-Villars, 1989
    41f. Portuguese edition:
         Lisbon: Instituto Piaget, 1994
    41g. Japanese edition:
         Sapporo: Aleph, Inc.

1988

42. **L'Ipotesi del Campo Psi**
    Bergamo: Pierluigi Lubrina Editore (in Italian)

1989

43. **Physis: Abitare La Terra**
    with Mauro Ceruti (edited)
    Milano: Feltrinelli

1991

44. **The New Evolutionary Paradigm**
    Keynote Volume of General Evolution Studies (edited)
    New York: Gordon and Breach

45. *The Age of Bifurcation*
    The Key to Understanding the Changing World
    New York and London: Gordon & Breach
      45a. German edition: *Global Denken*
           Rosenheim: Horizonte Verlag, 1988
      45b. German pocketbook edition:
           München: Goldmann Verlag, 1991
      45c. Spanish edition: *La Gran Bifurcacion*
           Barcelona: Gedisa Editorial, 1990
      45d. Chinese edition:
           Beijing: Chinese Academy of Social Sciences, 1990
      45e. French edition: *La Grande Bifurcation*
           Paris: Tacor International, 1990
      45f. Italian edition: *Il Pericolo E L'opportunita*
           Milano: Sperling, 1992
           Second edition:
           Rome: Aracne, 2008
      45g. Turkish edition:
           Istanbul: Isaret Yayinlari, 1992
           Second edition: 2004
      45h. Russian edition:
           Moskva: Put, 1995

1992

46. *New Lectures on Systems Philosophy*
    Beijing: Chinese Social Science Press (in Chinese)

47. *The Evolution of Cognitive Maps*
    New Paradigms for the 21st Century
    Proceedings of the Bologna Conference of the General Evolution
      Research Group
    with I. Masulli (edited)
    New York: Gordon & Breach

48. *Management By Evolution*
Global Thinking for Global Action
with Christopher Laszlo and Prince Alfred of Lichtenstein

    48a. German edition: *Evolutionäres Management*
        Fulda: Paidia Verlag, 1992
        Vienna: Der Standard, 1992

    48b. French edition: *Le Management Evolutionniste*
        Paris: Economica, 1993

    48c. Italian edition: *Navigare Nella Turbolenza*
        Milan: Franco Angeli, 1995

1993

49. *The Creative Cosmos*
Towards a Unified Science of Matter, Life, and Mind
Edinburgh: Floris Books

    49a. French edition: *Au Racines De L'Univers*
        Paris: Edition Fayard, 1992

    49b. Italian edition: *Alle Radice Dell'universo*
        Milano: Sperling Scienza, 1993

    49c German edition: *Kosmische Kreativität*
        Frankfurt, Insel Verlag, 1995

    49d. Chinese edition:
        Beijing: Chinese Academy of Social Sciences, 1994

    49e. Portuguese edition:
        Lisbon: Institut Piaget, 1994

    49f. Spanish edition: *El Cosmos Creativo*
        Barcelona: Kairos, 1997

50. *A Multicultural Planet*
Diversity and Dialogue in Our Common Future
Report of an Independent Expert Group to Unesco (edited)
Oxford: Oneworld, 1993

    50a. German edition: *Rettet Die Weltkulturen*
        Frankfurt: Horizonte Verlag 1993

    50b. Chinese edition:
        Beijing: Fujian People's Publishing House, 1997

1994

51. *Vision 2020*
Restructuring Chaos for Global Order
New York: Gordon & Breach
> 51a. Korean edition:
> Seoul: Minumsa Publishing Co., 1999
> 51b. Hungarian edition:
> Budapest: Magyar Könyvklub, 1999
> 51c. Kindle edition: Amazon, 2010

52. *The Choice: Evolution or Extinction*
The Thinking Person's Guide to Global Problems
Los Angeles: Tarcher/Putnam
> 52a. German edition: *Der Laszlo Report*
> München: Moderne Verlagsgesellschaft, 1992
> 52b. German pocketbook edition: *Der Laszlo Report*
> München: Wilhelm Heyne Verlag, 1994
> 52c. Chinese edition:
> Beijing and Taipei: SDX Joint Publishing Co., 1994
> 52d. Hungarian edition:
> Budapest: KIT Kiadó, 1994
> 52e. Korean edition:
> Seoul: Hankyore Publishing Co., 1994

1995

53. *Science and Reality*
German edition: *Wissenschaft Und Wirklichkeit*
> 53a. Frankfurt: Insel Verlag, 1995
> 53b. French edition: *Science Et Realité*
> Paris: du Rocher, 1996

54. *The Interconnected Universe*
Conceptual Foundations of Transdisciplinary Unified Theory
Singapore and London: World Scientific Ltd.

55. *Peace Through Dialogue*
    with Frank Schure (edited)
    German edition: *Frieden Durch Dialog*
    Berlin: Aufbau Verlag

1996

56. *Changing Visions*
    Human Cognitive Maps: Past, Present, and Future
    with Robert Artigiani, Allan Combs, and Vilmos Csányi
    Westport, CT: Praeger Publishers
    London: Adamantine Press

57. *The Whispering Pond*
    A Personal Guide to the Emerging Vision of Science
    Dorset, UK and Rockport, MA: Element Books
    Revised and enlarged edition: 1998

    57a. Brasilian edition:
        Sao Paolo: Editora Vozes, 2000
    57b. Hungarian edition:
        Budapest: Magyar Könyvklub, 1996
    57c. German edition:
        Bergisch-Gladbach: Lübbe Verlag, 2000
    57d. Japanese edition:
        Tokyo: Nippon Kyobunsha, 1999
    57e. Portuguese edition:
        Lisbon: Europa-America, 2000
    57f. Latvian edition:
        Riga: Madris 2004

58. *The Systems View of the World*
    A Holistic Vision for Our Time
    (revised and enlarged edition of #13)
    Cresskill, NJ: Hampton Press

    58a. German edition:
        München: Diederich Verlag, 1998

58b. Hungarian edition:
      Budapest: Magyar Könyvklub, 2000

59. *Evolution: The General Theory*
    (revised and enlarged edition of #41)
    Cresskill, NJ: Hampton Press

1997

60. *The Insight Edge*
    An Introduction to the Theory and Practice of Evolutionary
      Management with Christopher Laszlo
    Westport, CT: Quorum Books
      60a. German edition:
            Wiesbaden: Gabler Verlag, 1997

61. *The Concept of Collective Consciousness*
    Research Perspectives (edited)
    Special Issue of *World Futures*, 48:1–4

62. *Third Millenium: The Challenge and the Vision*
    London: Gaia Books
      62a. French edition:
            Paris: Village Mondial, 1997
      62b. Italian edition:
            Milan: Corbaccio, 1998
      62c. Chinese edition:
            Beijing: SDX Joint Publishing Co., 1998
      62d. Hungarian edition:
            Budapest: Uj Paradigma, 1998
      62e. German edition: *Aufbruch Ins Dritte Jahrtausend*
            Frankfurt: Suhrkamp Taschenbuch, 1998
      62f. Portuguese edition:
            Lisbon: Instituto Piaget, 1999
      62g. Russian edition:
            Moskva: Progress Tradition, 1999
      62f. Indonesian edition:
            Dinestindo Adiperkasa International, 2000

62e. Japanese edition:
       Tokyo: Sunchoch Publishing, 1999

1998

63. *L'uomo E L'universo*
     Rome: Di Renzo Editore (in Italian)

64. *Dialogue Across Continents Through the Centuries*
     The Century's Problems Focused on Systems Theory
     with Herman Haken and Wu Jie
     Beijing: The People's Press (in Chinese)

65. *The New Enterprise Culture*
     (edited)
     Special Issue of *World Futures*, 51:1–2

1999

66. *The Consciousness Revolution*
     A Transatlantic Dialogue
     with Stanislav Grof and Peter Russell
     Shaftesbury and Boston: Element Books
          66a. German edition:
                Frankfurt: Riemann Verlag, 1999
          66c. Hungarian edition:
                Budapest: Uj Paradigma, 1999
          66d. Chinese edition:
                Shanghai: SDX Joint Publishing Co., 1999
          66e. Spanish edition:
                Barcelona: Kairos Editorial, 2000
          66f. Italian edition:
                Rome: Editrice Nuova Era, 2003
          66g. Czech edition:
                Praha: Carpe Momentum, 2013
          66h. Korean edition:
                Seoul: Kyung Hee University Press, 2016

2001

67. *Macroshift*
Navigating the Transformation to a Sustainable World
San Francisco: Berret-Koehler

  67a. Japanese edition:
  Tokyo: Bunshun Nesco, 2002
  67b. Chinese complex characters edition:
  Locus Publishing Co. Taipei, 2002
  67c. Chinese simple characters edition:
  Beijing: Civic Publishing House, 2002
  67d. Dutch edition:
  Scriptum, Schiedam, 2002
  67e. French edition:
  Montreal & Paris:
  Les Editions de L'Homme, 2002
  67f. Portuguese-Brazilian edition:
  Sao Paolo: Axis Mundi, 2002
  67g. German edition:
  Franfurt: Insel Verlag, 2003
  67h. Turkish edition:
  Istanbul: Morpa Kultur Yayinlari, 2003
  67i. Russian edition:
  Moscow: Ecology & Life, 2004

2002

68. *Holos*
The World of the New Sciences

  68a. German edition:
  Petersberg: Via Nova
  68b. Italian edition:
  Milan: Editora Riza, 2003

69. *You Can Change the World*
Handbook for Responsible Thinking and Acting
London: Positive News

  69a. Hungarian edition:
  Budapest: Hungarian Book Club

70. *Your Life in a Macroshift*
    (children's edition of *Macroshift*)
    with Inty Mendoza and Walmir Cedotti
    Brazilian edition:
    Sao Paolo: Axis Mundi
       70a. Japanese edition:
          Tokyo: Artisthouse Publishers, 2003

2003

71. *You Can Change the World*
    The Global Citizen's Handbook for Living on Planet Earth
    (revised edition of #71)
    New York: Select Books
       71a. Japanese edition co-authored with Masami Saionji:
          Tokyo: Kawade Shobo Shinsha, 2003
       71b. Italian edition:
          Milano: Editora Riza, 2003
       71c. Dutch edition:
          Deventer: Ankh Hermes, 2004
       71d. Spanish edition:
          Madrid: Nawtilus, 2004
       71e. German edition:
          Berlin: Ullstein, 2005
       71f. French edition:
          Quebec: Ariane Editions, 2005
       71g. Portuguese edition:
          Lisbon, 2008
       71h. Czech edition:
          Prague: Malvern, 2010

72. *The Connectivity Hypothesis*
    Foundations of an Integral Science of Quantum, Cosmos, Life,
    and Consciousness
    Albany: State University of New York Press
       72a. Chinese edition:
          Beijing: Chinese Social Sciences Publishing House, 2004

2004

73. *Die Neugestaltung Der Vernetzten Welt*
    Global Denken—Global Handeln (in German)
    revised & updated edition of #45a
    Petersberg: Via Nova Verlag

74. **Science and the Akashic Field**
    An Integral Theory of Everything
    U.S./ North American edition:
    Rochester, VT: Inner Traditions International
    74a. Norwegian edition:
          Oslo: Flux, 2003
    74b. Dutch edition:
          Deventer: Ankh Hermes, 2004
    74c. Spanish edition:
          Madrid: Nawtilus, 2004
    74d. German edition:
          Berlin: Ullstein/Allegria, 2005
    74e. Chinese edition:
          Shanghai: CITIC, 2006
    74f. Japanese edition:
          Tokyo: Nihon-Kyobunsha, 2005
    74g. French edition:
          Quebec: Ariane Editions, 2005
    74h. Croatian edition:
          Zagreb: VBZ Publishers, 2006

2006

75. **Global Survival**
    The Challenge and Its Implications for Thinking and Acting
    with Peter Seidel (edited)
    New York: SelectBooks

76. **Science and the Reenchantment of the Cosmos**
    The Rise of the Integral Vision of Reality
    U.S./North American edition:
    Rochester, VT: Inner Traditions International

76a. Dutch edition:
Deventer: Ankh Hermes, 2005

76e. French edition:
Quebec, Ariane, 2005

76b. Norwegian edition:
Oslo: Flux, 2006

76c. Korean edition:
Seoul: Thinking Tree, 2006

76d. German edition:
Berlin: Ullstein/Allegria, 2006

76e. Italian edition:
Milan: Apogeo, 2007

76f. Russian edition:
Moscow: Ves Publishing, 2009

76g. Japanese edition:
Tokyo: Babel, 2009

77. The Chaos Point
The World at the Crossroads

77a. U.S./North American edition:
Charlottesville, VA: Hampton Roads

77b. UK edition:
London: Piatkus

77c. Hungarian edition:
Budapest: Kossuth Kiado, 2006

77d. Dutch edition:
Deventer: Ankh Hermes, 2006

77e. Japanese edition:
Tokyo: Nihon-Kyobunsha, 2006

79f. Hebrew edition:
Jerusalem: ARI, 2006 (with Michael Laitman)

77g. Russian edition:
Moscow: 2006 (with Michael Laitman)

77h. Korean edition:
Seoul: Thinking Tree, 2006

77i. German edition:
Berlin: Ekon Verlag, 2006

79j. Italian edition:
Milan: Apogeo, 2006/7

77k. Turkish edition:
      Istanbul: 2006
77l. French edition:
      Quebec: Ariane, 2007
77m. Brazilian (Portuguese) edition:
      San Paolo: Cultrix, 2008
77n. Russian edition:
      Moscow: Ves Publishing, 2009
77o. Chinese edition:
      Taiwan: Business Weekly Publications, 2011

2007

78. *Science and the Akashic Field*
    An Integral Theory of Everything
    Updated second edition
    Rochester, VT: Inner Traditions International
      78a. Norwegian edition:
            Oslo: Flux, 2007
      78b. Dutch edition:
            Deventer: Ankh Hermes, 2007
      78c. French edition:
            Quebec: Ariane, 2008
      78d. Italian edition:Milan: Apogeo, 2008
      78e. Brazilian (Portuguese) edition:
            San Paolo: Cultrix, 2008
      78f. Greek edition:
            Athens: 2008
      78g. Russian edition:
            Moscow: Ves Publishing, 2009
      78h. Romanian edition:
            Bucharest: Elena Francisc Publishing, 2009
      78i. Croatian edition:
            Zagreb: 2010
      78j. Latvian edition:
            Riga: Jumava, 2011

2008

79. *Quantum Shift in the Global Brain*
   How the New Scientific Reality Can Change Us and Our World
   Rochester, VT: Inner Traditions International
   79a. Japanese edition:
       Tokyo: Babel Press, 2008
   79b. Italian edition:
       Rome: Franco Angeli, 2008
   79c. Spanish edition:
       Barcelona: Kairos, 2009
   79d. Romanian edition:
       Bucharest: Elena Francisc Publishing, 2009
   79e. Russian edition:
       Moscow: Ves Publishing, 2009
   79f. Brazilian edition:
       San Paolo: Editora Pensamento Cultrix, 2009
   79g. Dutch edition:
       Deventer: Ankh Hermes, 2009
   79h. Latvian edition:
       Riga: Jumava, 2011
   79i. Chinese edition:
       Shanghai: Gold Wall Press, 2011

80. *Cosmos*
   The Co-Creators Guide to the Universe
   with Jude Currivan
   London and Carlsbad: Hay House 2008
   80a. Italian edition: Milan: Macroedizioni 2008
   80b. French edition:
       Quebec: Ariane, 2008/9
   80c. Dutch edition:
       Deventer: Ankh Hermes, 2009
   80d. Japanese edition:
       Tokyo: Kodansha, 2009
   80e. Brazilian edition:
       Sao Paolo: Pensamento-Cultrix, 2010
   80f. Romanian edition:
       Bucharest: Editura For You, 2011

2009

81. *The Akashic Experience*
    Science and the Cosmic Memory Field
    Rochester, VT: Inner Traditions International
    - 81a. Romanian edition:
      Bucharest: Elena Francisc Publishing
    - 81b. Dutch edition:
      Deventer: Ankh-Hermes
    - 81c. French edition:
      Paris: Editions Vega, 2013
    - 81d. Spanish edition:
      Barcelona: Editiones Obelisco, 2014

82. *Worldshift 2012*
    Making Green Business, New Politics and Higher Consciousness
      Work Together
    Rochester, VT: Inner Traditions International
    Toronto: McArthur & Co.
    - 82a. German edition:
      Munich: Scorpio Verlag 2009, 2011
    - 82b. Japanese edition:
      Tokyo: Bio Magazine
    - 82c. Hungarian edition:
      Budapest: Nyitott Konyvmuhely
    - 82d. Korean edition:
      Seoul: Darunwoori, 2010:
    - 82e. Chinese edition edition:
      Taiwan: Cite, 2011

2010

83. *Thomas Berry Dreamer of the Earth*
    The Spiritual Ecology of the Father of Envirnmentalism
    Edited with Allan Combs
    Rochester, VT: Inner Traditions

2011

84. **Simply Genius! And Other Tales from My Life**
   An Informal Autobiography, with a Foreword by Deepak Chopra
   Carlsbad, New York, London, Sidney: Hay House
   84a. Canadian edition:
       Toronto: MacArthur & Co
   84b. Korean edition:
       Seoul: Darunwoori
   84c. Dutch edition:
       Deventer: Ankh Hermes

85. **The Chaos Point 2012**
   Appointment with Destiny
   Revised & updated edition of #77
   85a. U.S./North American edition:
       Charlottesville, VA: Hampton Roads
   85b. UK edition:
       London: Little Brown & Co

2012

86. **The New Science and Spirituality Reader**
   Edited with Kingsley Dennis
   Rochester, VT: Inner Traditions International
   86a. Dutch edition:
       Deventer: Ankh Hermes
   86b. Italian edition:
       Isola del Liri: Editrice Pisani
   86c. Portuguese/Brazilian edition:
       Lisbon: Sinais de Fogo Publicacoes

87. **The Birth of the Akasha Paradigm**
   New Thinking for a New World
   i-book: Akashaparadigm.com

88. *The Akasha Paradigm in Science*
     (R)Evolution at the Cutting Edge
     e-book: Akashaparadigm.com

2013

89. *The Dawn of the Akashic Age*
     New Consciousness, Quantum Resonance, and the Future
       of the World
     with Kingsley Dennis
     Rochester, VT: Inner Traditions International

90. *Il Senso Ritrovato*
     with Pier Mario Biava
     Milano: Springer (in Italian)

2014

91. *Value Theory in Philosophy and Social Science*
     with J. Wilbur (edited)
     (new edition of #18)
     London: Routledge

92. *The Self-Actualizing Cosmos*
     The Akasha Revolution in Science and Human Consciousness
     Rochester, VT: Inner Traditions
        92a. Malayam edition:
              Kerala: State Institute of Languages

93. *The Immortal Mind*
     Science and the Continuity of Consciousness Beyond the Brain
     with Anthonyh Peake
     Rochester, VT: Inner Traditions
        93a. Spanish edition:
              Rochester, VT: Inner Traditions in Espagnol
        93b. German edition:
              Potsdam: Mosquito Verlag, 2016

93c. Italian edition:
      Vicenza: Il Punto d'Incontro, 2016
93d. Czech edition:
      Prague, 2016
93e. Hungarian edition:
      Budapest: Angyali Menedék, 2018

2016

94. **What Is Consciousness?**
     Three Sages Lift the Veil
     with Larry Dossey and Jean Houston
     New York: SelectBooks

95. **What Is Reality?**
     The New Map of Cosmos and Consciousness
     with Alexander Laszlo
     New York: SelectBooks

2017

96. **Beyond Fear and Rage**
     New Light from the Frontiers of Science and Spirituality (edited)
     Waterfront Press (e-book)

2018

97. **The Intelligence of the Cosmos**
     Why Are We Here?—*New Answers from the Frontiers of Science*
     With an Introduction by Jane Goodall and Afterword by James O'Dea
     Contributions by Emanuel Kuntzelman, Kingsley Dennis,
         Maria Sagi, et al.
     Rochester, VT: Inner Traditions
         96a. Hungarian edition:
               Budapest: Angyali Menedék, 2018
         96b. Chinese edition (in preparation)

2019

98. *Information Medicine*
with Pier Mario Biava
Rochester, VT: Inner Traditions

99. *The Tuscany Dialogues*
with Michael Charles Tobias
New York: SelectBooks/EcoPrime Publications

2020

100. *Reconnecting to the Source*
The New Science of Spiritual Experience:
How It Can Change You; How It Can Transform The World
New York: St. Martin's Press

101. *Global Shift Now!*
A Call to Evolution
Waterside Productions

102. *How We Can Build a Better World*
The Worldshift Manual
Waterside Productions

2021

103. *The Immutable Laws of the Askashic Field*
Connecting Cutting-Edge Science with Classical Wisdom
New York: St. Martin's Press

104. *Dawn of the Era of Wellbeing*
with Frederick Tsao
New York: SelectBooks/EcoPrime Publications

105. *My Journey*
     A Life in Quest of the Purpose of Life
     New York: SelectBooks/EcoPrime Publications
     and Waterside Productions

106. *The Wisdom Principles*
     A Handbook of Timeless Truths and Timely Wisdom
     New York: St. Martin's Press

Index